LEADERSHIP MAGIC

Conjuring up simple
solutions to drive change

by Business Coach

Grahame Pitts

Tales from the boardroom for
leaders and influencers

Praise for Leadership Magic

"Leadership Magic is one of those special business books that you will go back to again and again. If you have run out of options and are searching for that a-ha moment or need a conversation starter with your team, this is your book – the business challenges are relatable, the fables are clever – providing new perspectives – and best of all, the learnings are instant. Try it."

Aoife Beirne, Deputy CEO

"I was touched that Grahame wanted to use me for his stories. Unfortunately, even now, few women run companies. I believe a key reason is the overwhelming task of managing not one but two sets of plates for your personal and professional life. It takes a lot of energy and positivity to keep both sets spinning. But visualising the plates and the 'power of three' helps focus the mind and clarify the most important jobs at work and home. It empowers you and the people around you to find a consensus on which big plates you need to work on together to spin.

Technology now allows for overwhelming multiple-channel communication (email, phone calls, texts, WhatsApp, Teams, dual or even triple screening), which means that the everyday to-do list has only gotten larger and more unwieldy. Being able to focus on those plates which will bring about the most positive change and successful business results is even more important.

Turning the plates shiny gold, giving them more oxygen and light while eliminating the timewasters, makes me feel psychologically better. Like shedding extra layers of clothing and only wearing things that make me and the team fly."

Teresa Arbuckle, CEO

"Grahame helped me find the tools and stories within me and realise that I may need to reverse backwards before driving forwards to find the right road again. Thankfully I am back on the right road now, even if the running shoes have been in the cupboard for a while! Despite the pain I went *through, I can see now how these learnings have made me stronger whilst not taking so many things for granted as I had perhaps done in the past."*

James Anon, Sales Director

"I liken Grahame's fables to the stories of battle honours in the army. We won because our attitude was strong. Although outnumbered and outgunned, we fought on. Every Para will know the acronym of the regimental battle honours: 'BRAB AN TOPS' (you can test me anytime). The names and events are rammed into your brain in training. Why? To give you a sense of Esprit de Corps and that you know how to approach every situation you face. And it works."

Nigel Smith, Finance Operations Director

"I really enjoyed reading 'Something's Moving in the Garden' again. When you shared it with me originally, it resonated on many levels. I recognised the attractiveness of my business

proposition had changed in some people's eyes as it grew into something bigger and quite likely somewhat different to what they had envisaged. It helped me see that some perceived it as a risk – or a threat. Whereas I was proud to have turned an idea I believed in into a successful business and was tired of continuously having to convince others of its merits and defend its differences, I also realised my 'dragon' had grown up and would survive with or without me. It has!"

Dame Jo da Silva DBE,
Global Sustainable Development Director

"*In our western society, work is often seen as an 'artificial life', or at least a 'disconnected life', and most people feel they need to be, behave or think differently to how they do in the rest of their life. The expression 'work/life balance' instead of 'work/home balance' illustrates the point.*

Then, because work is disconnected from other life, people sometimes cannot think or act with the conviction that they do it elsewhere. Stories, especially analogies, help people bridge a world they understand and readily relate to with a world they feel less comfortable with. When someone gets the story, they invariably get clarity on the work situation. What's more, the language in the story is safe, and often the reference points live on and have value long after the story has been told."

David Alexander, CEO

"*When Grahame sent me his fable to re-read and write something about for the book, I was probably somewhere in between the first punch and* the garden, in need of a pep talk and a tomato. I had taken a few knocks recently and wasn't feeling very creative, so I left the email unread for a few weeks. On finally building the courage to tackle the task, I was overcome by the power of the story – just as I was five years ago when Grahame first showed it to me. 'Knockout Fight' perfectly captures today, just as it did back then, the often-overwhelming rollercoaster of a challenge that is pursuing a dream. You want it to be a linear rise towards success, but the reality is you'll get knocked down, again and again, learning something each time. Eventually, if you stay in the game and find ways to take down each opponent, the win finally comes.

I've been lucky enough to mentor a younger talent myself recently, and as I said to him, the most challenging opponents you'll come across in an artistic career are all inside your head. They are all the boxer, as in the story, representing different negative emotions that you can either let overwhelm and knock you out or dodge, duck, dip, dive and dodge your way past to victory.

I can never overstate Grahame's powerful impact on me and my career. He's a true friend and a man with an incredible gift of releasing pressure in any situation. As with all good mentors, he rarely tells you exactly what you need to do, instead guiding you to find the answer within the whole time – like some kind of therapeutic snake charmer. That ability to illuminate the facts and hold up a metaphorical mirror to enable someone to see themselves is a rare talent that I know all who've benefitted from working with Grahame are grateful that he nurtured.

I hope 'Knockout Fight' and the other wonderful fables help others pursue a career that utilises their talents. It can be the most challenging pursuit, but ultimately the rewards for not giving up are immense."

Joe Hicks, Singer-Songwriter

"I think the story is brilliant! 'Groundless Ground' vividly shows the great challenge of leadership: how to take risks, boldly but not recklessly, and to use the wisdom of teams with diverse views to move forward. In reflection, I would add to the story by highlighting more the role of the team: diversity is absolutely essential to bring different perspectives to all groups. Ask yourself and others: 'How do I best imagine the future? Am I an analyst, an explorer, a dreamer, a survivor?' And be true to your style."

David McRedmond, Chairman & CEO

"I worked with Grahame over several years as he helped me work through the many stages of transition of growing my business from a 'kitchen table' operation to a successful market-leading consultancy. From the first session, I connected with Grahame and his use of storytelling and visual images to stimulate reflection; they helped me see and work through challenges. Grahame has an extraordinarily high level of insight that he manages to capture in his stories, stimulating deep, lateral reflections and personal insights that I don't think I would have arrived at through regular coaching. I personally enjoyed his use of visual images, which prompted a period of sharing postcards with each other. 'Not all who wander are lost' was a great one for helping me understand the journey to exiting my company was not fruitless but incredibly fruitful. I thought I was lost in a quagmire at the time, and that *particular postcard helped me to see that it was all part of the journey that inspired me to final clarity and action. The 'relaxed cat' (on its back on a sheepskin rug) provoked a discussion about the feelings it evoked and again prompted clarity for both personal and professional decisions. It still sits on my mantlepiece as a proud reminder of what I have achieved."*

Sue Philips, Social Entrepreneur

"I have been privileged and lucky enough to work with Grahame over the last twenty-five years on leadership and development strategy. The situations and organisations might differ, but the key takeaways are consistent – the need to be an authentic and empathetic leader. A leader recognises what each individual brings and puts as much effort into effective team dynamics as they do strategy. It is about authentically living the vision and values to create the energy and engagement to drive success."

Cindy Rampersaud, MD & Non-Executive Director

"Unlike many business texts that promote the formulaic implementation of dry theoretical frameworks, Grahame's collection talks to the heart and humanity of getting business done with a mixture of thought-provoking relatable stories relevant for any experienced or future leader."

Ben Wishart, Global Chief Information Director

LEADERSHIP MAGIC

Conjuring up simple
solutions to drive change

Text and illustrations © Grahame Pitts 2023

All rights reserved. No part of this publication may be reproduced, distributed, or transmitted in any form or by any means, including photocopying, recording, or other electronic or mechanical methods, without the prior written permission of the publisher, except in the case of brief quotations embodied in reviews and certain other non-commercial uses permitted by copyright law.

ISBN 978-1-4478-4792-2

www.grahamepitts.co.uk

This book is dedicated to everyone who wants to learn, change and help others to do so too.

*Enjoy your adventure.
I hope this book takes you one more step on your journey.*

Contents

15 Introduction
Finding a New Narrative

21 Chapter One
Purple Armour: Developing Self-Protection

33 Chapter Two
Spinning Plates: Prioritising High Value

43 Chapter Three
Groundless Ground: New Opportunities

59 Chapter Four
Power Surge: Impact and Effectiveness

71 Chapter Five
James Goes Running: Being Resourceful

83 Chapter Six
Knockout Fight: Self-Belief

97 Chapter Seven
Something's Moving in the Garden: Difference

113 Chapter Eight
The Crucible: Difficult Conversations

125 Chapter Nine
Canoe Trip: Expecting Change

137 Final Thoughts
A Day at the Office

140 Acknowledgements

141 About the Author

INTRODUCTION
Finding a New Narrative

Recently, I was speaking to a CEO about developing talent. He used the metaphor of a young eagle beginning to fly. How the eagle's natural wingspan widens as the bird grows, allowing higher, broader flight and, as a result, catching more thermals – lifting and flying even further. That was why he wanted young talent in his business – to capture all the available thermals. The metaphor stuck with me and it is the essence of this short book.

My work over the last thirty years has taken me into organisations big and small, meeting leaders and influencers, individuals wanting to make a difference – and really doing that. As a business coach, or – as one of my clients describes me – "my business therapist", I have been asked to help resolve many different situations and issues. Some are clear, rational and easy to understand. Others are more complex, emotional, difficult to decipher and often painful for all concerned. Then, ten years ago, I worked with a HR director struggling with an ineffective board and a bullying chairman. We discussed putting on psychological armour, and this became my first business story, Purple Armour, which brought a new perspective, a different angle, on a recurring problem. This book has come as a result of this and other experiences – rather more by accumulation than intent – a set of different scenes fitting together in a pattern I wanted to share with you.

> "I write stories to help me understand what is happening to people and organisations, particularly leaders and key influencers."

Stories have always been important to me, although I came to writing late in my career. I can build a narrative and often use metaphors in my work, but writing stories was a desire to understand a situation, and represent and see things differently. Initially, I did this for myself, writing about my life when I had a frighteningly powerful experience. I found a different perspective and deeper insight when I reflected and wrote about it later.

Now I write stories to help me understand what is happening to people and organisations, particularly leaders and key influencers. Some situations are obvious and clear and need just a first step forwards, an action. Some, though, require more thought and reflection. Writing down my thoughts and thinking them through as I write helps me. I often see a person or the question they face differently and encourage them metaphorically through my writing. Initially,

Finding a New Narrative

I did this just to open up a problem for myself, to find a way to coach and support someone through a roadblock. Sometimes, just to describe, to express and release the confusion, spiralling energy, anger and doubt at what they were experiencing. Or, on the reverse side, to affirm the hope, passion and desire for movement and success. Either way, writing helped me see a new perspective and a possible way forward. After sharing Purple Armour with that HR director, I discovered this helped them too.

Life, or leadership, stories articulated differently can provide fresh insight on a specific question or an issue and some point to more general life truths. I know this from my daily work in organisations. They offer a new way of seeing, noticing or learning about a situation, particularly for those that are stuck and need some help to reframe a problem.

I have seen knots can become untangled and moments of clarity or magic occur after the hard work of reflection, review and learning. Literally sometimes leadership magic does happen.

> "Life, or leadership, stories articulated differently can provide fresh insight on a specific question or an issue and some point to more general life truths."

Enjoy these stories. To get the most from them, you may need to suspend your rational brain and be willing to go on a journey with me. Rest assured, each one has a firm base in daily reality, and its source was a real-life business situation and returns there at the close. You'll also find a list of suggested prompts

Leadership Magic

and possible actions at the end of each section. Enjoy your thinking and analysis, then follow your energy to go and deliver the results you want.

You can read this book from start to finish or go straight to the issue that interests you. Or you can even use my favourite method, which is to go in randomly and enjoy the direction you are pulled towards from there. Whichever route you choose, take the opportunity to make notes as you travel through, reflect on your current challenges and maybe consider new ways of looking at the questions you are facing. Let metaphors, connections and new insights help you. This is something that really does multiply the learning and allows us to capture the thermals around us.

"Knowing yourself is the beginning of all wisdom."

~ Aristotle, Philosopher

CHAPTER ONE
Purple Armour

> Protect yourself and your leadership while remaining open and taking in new information and possibilities. Find your style, approach, strength and how to look after yourself well.

The sun is warm coming in through the window, and the birds are chirping. The gardener passes, the mower briefly interrupting our conversation, sending a waft of grass cuttings and two-stroke exhaust fumes towards us. It should be a good day, away from the business, but Di is angry. I know her well; we have worked together on and off for several years. She works incredibly hard, I think too hard, but delivers amazing results, her team regularly wins awards, and they are benchmarked at the top in their field.

Di tells me about the board she sits on and the leadership team for the overall business. Her passion, belief and drive shine through her anger. She cares deeply. Her values, which she won't compromise, frame all her work. It seems to get personal quickly. Maybe she cares too much. Criticism seems to come her way in board meetings. Others are projecting blame onto her functional team. The attackers are primarily male, and the CEO has traits which can be perceived as bullying on a bad day. Emotional intelligence is low in the team. Di knows it is not all about them, though. Yes, they *do* need to change, and she recognises she needs it too. As we sip our coffee, we chat about protecting ourselves, not taking comments personally and letting information in but remaining strong, sure, and confident. We talk about armour . . .

Purple Armour: Developing Self-Protection

The packaging lay strewn on the office floor – cardboard, string and tissue thrown aside.

Christina did a little spin and chuckled to herself. It was a good fit, made to her measurements, of course. Super lightweight, too, so not heavy at all. Some new-fangled material and pale purple, her favourite. Looking over her shoulder to check the door was shut, Christina turned around, doing a slow spin before dipping back into the box and pulling out the matching boots and gloves. A warm glow seeped through her as she pulled on each one.

A tap at the door pulled her back. Marcus, her PA, poked his head around the door, reminding her of her next meeting – one of the last before the Christmas break. Christina took

Purple Armour

the final item from the box and, sliding it under her arm, grabbed her notes and headed out into the corridor. The whole thing made her giggle, but all she showed as she walked along was a relaxed smile. Then a wave of concern swept over her. She shouldn't feel like this, not this at ease. Today was the executive meeting, and usually, no matter how much preparation she did, she felt uneasy. Not that she was alone in this, but no one talked about it, no one dared. George, her boss, was tough, very tough and as the sales slipped, almost a bully. He wouldn't describe it like that, "demanding," he called it, but Christina had felt his wrath on more than one occasion, and it wasn't pleasant or necessary. Worse, it had now begun to eat at her self-confidence so that she exposed her usual, sharp, incisive approach less and less nowadays.

Five minutes early for the meeting, Christina slipped into the restroom next to the boardroom. So, here is the big test, she thought as she made final adjustments to her outfit and pulled on the headgear. The helmet fitted snugly to her head, and immediately she felt the warm lining, purple-coloured, of course, lying softly against her skin. She raised her hands and pulled the visor down. It clicked softly shut, and the world disappeared. Straight away felt protected, yet she could hear, more sharply than usual, the sounds of people chatting next door as they arrived for the meeting.

She picked up her folder from the top of the washbasin and glanced at herself in the mirror. A fully uniformed knight looked back, complete with magnificent armour, glowing in the low

Leadership Magic

bathroom light. She nodded, and he nodded back, mirroring her movements. The light glinted on her suit filling the whole room with a powerful light. Could it be her? Surely not. This was a six-foot-plus, broad-chested person, resplendent in strength and confidence – a battle-strong, confident warrior. They appraised each other over the washbasin and then, with a final nod, set off.

Christina walked into the boardroom and took her usual place beside the company secretary, one of the good guys. Nothing was different. Certainly, grumpy George was grumpy. Worse, really, he'd just had sight of this week's sales figures and was taking this out on Isaac, the Operations Director. Not a good start. Others were shuffling papers, looking away, avoiding the apparent conflict at the head of the table.

Inside her armour, Christina felt calm, sliding into an observer role. Interestingly, none of the pain spewing from the gap between George and Isaac affected her. What a relief the armour works, she thought, settling comfortably in her chair, enjoying her filter coffee.

Isaac turned his head down the table, a look of desperation on his strained red face, beads of sweat running down his cheeks. All eyes were on papers, coffee cups, phones and laptops – no one met his gaze in return. Christina didn't want to either. It was eight-thirty in the morning, the armour was untested, and she didn't have the strength to take on George. She felt her hands on her visor. Yes, it was shut. Yes, she was safe. She could ride out the storm with her feelings protected.

Isaac's head dropped as no support came from the team.

Purple Armour

Inside Christina, a different feeling began to rise – anger, indignant anger and a sense of love and care for the team and for the business. She tried to push these down, knowing the result would be conflict. Her mother always said she had strong views and values even as a young kid, and these would bring her endless joy and plenty of heartaches. Oh dear, her heart was certainly aching here. It wasn't her battle, she tried to say to herself. Stay out of it. Isaac's a tough cookie. He'll handle it.

Even as Christina thought those words, she felt herself move. She stood up, and her armour began to glow and sparkle. Eyes turned towards her with many surprised looks. She pushed back her chair and, with one nimble leap, jumped onto the old boardroom table. Her helmet smashed against the chandelier, wafting years of dust across the room.

Christina, the knight, towered above the others in the room, and she saw her mate Cyril, the company secretary, looking across the table and smiling.

> "Inside her armour, Christina felt calm, sliding into an observer role."

Christina imagined him seeing a beautiful pair of crafted steel boots planted there among the coffee cups, glasses and water bottles. Then looking up to see the intricate panels and details of her armour. Right up to the helmet, gently tapping against the still swinging chandelier. Cyril's eyes ran back down and stopped at the sword, not drawn yet but with a gloved hand on the hilt, ready for action. He reached out and placed an affectionate hand on

Leadership Magic

the metal foot. The boot responded with a slight upturn of the pointed toe and then a tap back down.

George, in full flight, his tongue lashing full pelt at Isaac, saw none of this, but he did notice the tremor of the table as Christina walked towards him. Team members pulled their papers and coffees hastily out of the way. Geoff from Logistics was a little slow, and Christina inadvertently stood on his phone, sending bits flying across the polished tabletop. George did notice the dust, and later, he would vaguely wonder about where it came from, but what he really noticed and felt there and then was the large steel pointy purple boot which placed itself against his chest from belly button to throat, pressing him back and downwards into his fine black leather chair.

> "Inside her suit, she felt powerful and strong, yet strangely humble. The knight had delivered his message. No more was needed."

The knight stood in front of George, looking down at him, one foot placed squarely on the minutes of the last meeting, the other planted firmly on the CEO's chest. George's eyes grew wider and wider as he watched the knight release a jewel-encrusted sword from its scabbard. His throat was dry and not from the two cups of early morning coffee but from the fear welling up inside of him. He tried to summon up the spittle to speak. He couldn't. His lips moved; they formed the words, yet nothing appeared. Instead, it was his turn to sweat – and he did. Rivers ran down his face, pouring

Purple Armour

through his hair, soaking down into his collar and creating a tideline across his shirt.

Christina looked at him through her visor. The sword slid back into its scabbard. Inside her suit, she felt powerful and strong, yet strangely humble. The knight had delivered his message. No more was needed. She turned back down the table, dropped gently to the floor and strode out of the room, leaving the door open. Everyone observed her striding down the length of the executive corridor towards the lift. As she walked, she waved to the wide-eyed office staff, who grabbed onto each other, or their desks, in both fear and delight.

The Christmas break that followed was, for Cyril, a time for smiling and remembering old adventures – defeats and victories. Isaac mostly slept but came back in January refreshed. George had some nightmares and reflected a great deal. He found he got confused, remembering dust floating from the chandelier and feeling the tension in his chest. Yet he was gentle and loving with his children and grandchildren on Christmas day. For Christina, the world was simply a brighter place, full of new opportunities and promises, waiting to be lived to her own values. And in her wardrobe hung a beautiful purple suit of armour, shimmering in the half-light, ready and waiting.

Leadership Magic

Protect Yourself, Put on Your Psychological Amour

I watched Di expand and grow as she wore her armour more regularly. Of course, it didn't solve every problem, but it helped in several situations. Some of us will, by nature, always open ourselves to others when perhaps we should be protecting ourselves a little more. We want to connect with colleagues; it is a very natural process. Sadly though, sometimes, others can't stop themselves from seeing this "openness" and exploiting the situation, often unconsciously. This seems like an external problem: *What are they doing to me? Why are they so aggressive? Why don't they stop?*

A percentage of this is about the other person and the overall situation. But perhaps the first step in dealing with it is to manage our response to what is happening. The concept of psychological armour, the ability to protect ourselves, is available to everyone regardless of the circumstance. This internal protection will result in changes and different outward approaches. This starts as an inner personal resolve, a willingness and decision to notice the impact a potentially hostile world can have on us. Then having noticed this impact, only allowing in – through the filters in our armour – information which helps us. You don't withdraw; it is not the classic fight-fight-freeze response. We are still in the conversation,

> "The concept of psychological armour, the ability to protect ourselves, is available to everyone regardless of the circumstance."

Purple Armour

still there in the room, but we aim to protect ourselves from damaging comments. This new approach, a small shift, gives us more resources, perhaps even the ability, if we choose, to metaphorically walk down the boardroom table and put a foot on the CEO's chest. Remember to wear your psychological armour daily. It's a beneficial leadership resource.

Prompts and Actions

What in this story has meaning for you?
Where did you find yourself pulled towards as you were reading – the overall situation, a particular character, the outcome or something else?

Do you look after yourself well, particularly in challenging situations?
Do you have good psychological armour when needed? When you have your visor down, can you still listen to incoming information, protect yourself and engage in connected leadership?

How well do you know yourself?
Do you know the triggers which impact the quality of your capability, resourcefulness and energy? When you are driving change for yourself or others, are you over-armoured, under-armoured, or wearing just the right amount? Does anything need to change?

"Stories are how we remember; we tend to forget lists and bullet points"

~ Robert McKee, *Storynomics* Author, Speaker

CHAPTER TWO

Spinning Plates

> Find high-value areas for yourself and others. Be willing to prioritise and focus on the key few – those that truly make the difference for you and your business.

The clock is ticking. Another minute passes, and the Operations Director and I look at each other. We have already lost a third of our planning work time. He sighs and heads back to his emails, taking the opportunity to catch up. His fingers rap down on the keyboard. We made a mistake booking our meeting with the CEO for the late afternoon. By this stage, we know Teresa will be running late. Every meeting is important, and trading is tough. She arrives in a rush, apologising and then pauses for a moment to look out of the huge porthole window; the traffic is beginning to stream out of the business park as people head for home. Her phone goes off, and she mouths apologies as she takes the call. Finally, we sit together and begin our planning . . .

Spinning Plates: Prioritising High Value

"Where do you want 'em, boss? Some pretty ones here, not just those plain old white ones. We seem to have hundreds of them." Joe, the Facilities Manager, added the plates to the pile by the door of the CEO's office, smiled at what he saw, felt slightly confused about it all, then picked up the old boxes and headed back to the warehouse.

Caroline, the CEO, heard him and waved but hadn't time to stop – too much going on. Life had been manic since her promotion, a whirlwind of meetings, decisions and financial information. She grabbed another plate and, with a flick of her wrist, added it to the others already spinning around her.

Some in the office thought it was an art installation. Others thought it was a new keep-fit regime. Some believed Caroline had shares in a homeware factory. It was, though, they all agreed, an amazing sight. Endless plates spun in the sunlight, the canes supporting them wiggling and bending as they held the centre of gravity. And better still was the skill, grace and determination that Caroline displayed in moving quickly and confidently between them, occasionally giving some an additional twist to keep them spinning. She hummed to herself, occasionally doing a light jig as she went about her work.

Plates spun in her office, out in the open-plan office and now in the service centre too. Caroline had to pay special attention there, as phone calls to customers were key, and any plates crashing to the floor would have been disastrous. Roger, the Service Manager, had taken to giving the wobbliest plates a spin. He knew what spinning plates were like. He'd

Spinning Plates

had years of experience, and when he thought Caroline wasn't looking, he lifted one or two plates from their poles and hid them in a cupboard. Endless plates spun in the sunlight, the canes supporting them wiggling and bending as they held the centre of gravity.

"A head office plate has just arrived," called Lana, the PA, through the maze of sticks around her. Caroline turned her head, and sure enough, Lana was just taking a large hand-painted plate from a jiffy bag and holding it out to her.

"Okay, wait, wait, let's just clear a space, and we'll get it going." Between them, they shifted the other plates around a little. Then with

> "Endless plates spun in the sunlight, the canes supporting them wiggling and bending as they held the centre of gravity."

one huge throw of her arm and with assistance from Debbie, the Finance Director who'd just arrived, holding the stick, the plate began to spin. Everyone held their breath. The plate twisted and slipped on the pole with a screech, but with the combined energy of Lana, Debbie and Caroline working together and wiggling the stick, they got it centred, and it began to spin and whirr in the air.

Caroline reflected: Not bad, not bad at all, and provided she didn't take a lunch break, stayed late and came in at weekends, it seemed to be working. Which was why, as she took a quick sip of her cold coffee, she didn't appreciate HR Director Geoff's quiet, reflective comment: "Have you noticed how some of the plates seem more interesting than others?"

Leadership Magic

She muttered under her breath at the interruption but made herself stop and look around. Geoff was right. Some did seem more colourful and almost cried out for more space to spin. Caroline walked about under the plates looking up at them carefully, finding herself attracted to certain designs, shapes and sizes. Not all were huge by any means. Of course, the head office one was. They all knew it had to be there and needed constant spinning.

Lana brought her another coffee, and as she sipped it and munched her favourite chocolate biscuits, she considered each one. Then she made a decision, and sometimes alone, other times in consultation with her executive team – who had also been summoned to look at the plates – she began to pull some out, neatly taking each unwanted

> "Adding a twist to a pole now and then, watching as each plate seemed to change and grow in the sunlight."

plate and pole and putting it aside. First, the small side plates, then the ordinary white dinner plates. As they went, her heart lifted a little. Joe was hastily summoned, and he repacked the unwanted ones into boxes and placed them on his trolley. She ignored the coughs, the taps on the office door, the muttered comments – "That was my plate, it's very important in my department, you know" or "Wrong call, you'll regret that" – and went about her work. Adding a twist to a pole now and then, watching as each plate seemed to change and grow in the sunlight.

Soon there were just a few beautiful plates spinning, and

Spinning Plates

beside each one, a director stood, occasionally wiggling the stick. Caroline walked around them all, checking they had the right ones, moving at the right speed, adding a twist to a pole now and then, watching as each plate seemed to change and grow in the sunlight. To her amazement, one or two slowly turned a golden colour, with beautiful embossing appearing around the edges, and now these plates almost seemed to spin by themselves.

"Well, would you look at that," said Geoff, pointing to the head office plate. It still spun rapidly, but now it was smaller, not quite such a bright colour, almost drawing less attention. The executive team laughed together as they watched the Finance Director niftily reposition his plate near the golden ones, and there they continued to spin very happily together.

The white plates were later used on the "smash the crockery" stall at the next family fun day. Roger owned up to the plates in his cupboard, and his judgement was shown to be pretty good, apart from one small plate with some interesting swirls of colour in the design. Some senior managers kept this one spinning and found it was a potential winner for next year's budget.

Caroline got home early some days, leaving others spinning plates, knowing when to intervene and using her energy and skills wisely. And it made her smile when visitors to the business asked to see the plates, particularly the golden ones. Sometimes she showed them. At other times, she talked about confidentiality and went about her business with a spring in her step. Head Office seemed pretty satisfied too.

Leadership Magic

Setting Priorities on High-Value Items

I have never met a leader with too little to do. Even when things are going well, and they could take some downtime, most don't. They continue to look for more possibilities, develop new ideas, find ways to help colleagues, provide new products and shape a better world. This is exciting and interesting work, but there is a problem. Sometimes we take on so much that we endlessly move from one task to the next, keeping everything and everyone engaged and energised. Sometimes, just "spinning plates". This can be exhausting for you and for others around you, and can eventually be debilitating and stressful for individuals, teams and for a whole organisation.

The most successful leaders differentiate between valuable items (there are always many) and highly valuable items (those that really change a business or situation). Often everything seems very important, but these leaders can spot the critical activities which will give the most return on the investment in the broadest sense (energy, time, commitment, resources, money, etc.). One CEO I work with talks of the power of three. Focus on the three big key items. The rest can drop in behind these. It seems to work. Each business he has led has been highly successful.

"Focus on the three big key items. The rest can drop in behind these."

The difficulty is making a choice, deciding on one route rather than another. We will never know for sure if we have made the right choice. There is and always will be another path – actually, many paths. However, the results and the practical outcomes we see help us to stay on track – noticing what is working and why. And, of course, with any decision, we can always go back and test out another idea or approach (try another plate) if the first great idea isn't working.

Leadership Magic

Prompts and Actions

How many plates are you spinning in your business and life? Are there a few high-value ones which require more attention than others? How do you choose these?

Where do you need to show courage? Is there one plate that needs your particular focus and attention right now? Do you need to say "no" to others that might distract you?

If you lead a team, who needs to attend to which plate? Where might you delegate, and how? What do you need to do to allow those particular plates to become rich in colour or even turn to gold?

Where else in the organisation are there plates, perhaps hidden, which need finding and spinning? Which others may need stacking in the cupboard for now?

"The secret of change is to focus all your energy not on fighting the old but on building the new."

~ Socrates, Father of Western Philosophy

CHAPTER THREE

Groundless Ground

> The groundless ground is at the edge of change. Be willing to move forward on good and bad days. The adventure will happen, and richness will appear.

"We've got to move forwards, or this business is dead," David, the CEO, says, pushing his papers aside and staring at the executive team. Frustration is apparent from the way he leans forwards and gesticulates and how the team respond to his comments. Tired eyes look away up at the grand paintings on the wall or down to the highly patterned carpet in the conference room.

"I think we've done some good work. Look, we've stabilised the business, got the debt under control, renegotiated with suppliers, bought ourselves some time," he continues, looking around.

The Finance Director isn't afraid to speak up, though. He

Leadership Magic

faces the CEO squarely as he speaks. They eyeball each other across the table. "Yes, David, we've bought ourselves a year maybe, but after that . . . what happens? Do we really have a future? Honestly?"

The team look at each other. I'm not much help. I can't see a way through either or find a good facilitator's question to help them at this point in the meeting. They're all working hard, putting in long days and trying to build a new foundation for the business. The two days offsite have gone pretty well, but the last statement seems to suck the air out of the room. David takes off his dark-rimmed glasses. "Okay, enough for today. If there's a way, we'll find it. I've seen it before. So, get your antenna up. It will likely be unexpected, something beyond what we're doing now."

Groundless Ground: New Opportunities

The snow settled on the peak of his all-purpose balaclava as Jack studied his compass in the last light of the day. The worst of the storm was over, but he knew more was coming, the air too quiet and heavy. He shivered and felt his bones and muscles move and complain. The compass needle wavered, refusing to settle. Jack snapped the case shut and admitted the reality to himself. He'd told his team the direction was clear, the compass sure. This was good leadership rhetoric, but he suspected it would hold no more credence. Now the food was running low, and winter settling in.

Groundless Ground

They'd left with so much hope and expectation. A great adventure had been planned, seeking gold and riches to be found beyond the hills, in a land of plenty, they thought, with green fields and bountiful crops. They were the talk of the houses and pubs before they left. The hope and desire to find something they no longer had themselves. Their lands were barren, the water fetid,

> "People laughed about the strange ones, and it took all of Jack's communication skills to convince the King's advisors to take those with him."

taken from wells where the water table was wasting away. So the King supported Jack in taking the best the kingdom could provide, the elite of all the men and women. Not just the physical best, the brightest brains, the most creative and some of the strangest ones. People laughed about the strange ones, and it took all of Jack's communication skills to convince the King's advisors to take those with him.

One, Isof the Demolition, had just been released from jail for creating a magnificent mega firework, the best to explode over the city, which sadly landed on the Chancellor's house, burning a large hole in his smartly combed thatched roof. Those same skills, though, had been very handy when a marauding hill tribe rode into camp one night, screaming, swords waving, slashing tents. By the time Jack had grabbed his gun and pulled back the tent flap, the screams had turned to whimpers as a huge burst of light, sparks, smoke and noise erupted from the campfire. Isof, sharp, smart, undisciplined, always late for daily inspections but ready with unusual solutions anytime, had thrown a mega starburst firework (homemade, in his girlfriend's garden shed) onto the smouldering embers. The resulting explosion removed the helmet of the leading attacker, singed his eyebrows and sent him and his horse hurtling into the darkness. Dust flew around the remaining riders, causing a sooty smog where no one was sure who was who.

One of Jack's soldiers, making the most of this, jabbed his sword into his best mate, who'd just that evening taken a week's wages off him in a dice game. The following morning they would discover a metre-deep hole where the fire had been, which intrigued Isof and scared the rest of the troop witless. From that point, they refused to march next to him, let alone shoulder the sacks he carried.

One attack, one explosion, seemed to be enough, and no other attackers chanced their luck. Now Jack wished for a bit of distraction – anything to take his mind off what lay in the future. A good fight, anything rather than this endless trudging. Looking ahead through the steadily falling light snow, the track seemed to disappear, which wasn't surprising as the edge of the map had also disappeared two days ago.

Jasmine, his second in command, turned the map over and began drawing a new one on the other side, amongst the notes, lists and mullings Jack had been recording during

> "Looking ahead through the steadily falling light snow, the track seemed to disappear."

Groundless Ground

their time on the road. They now had a new map for the cartographers to work with when they got back, including a set of hills named "Food I'll Eat", after a mouth-watering list Jack made one evening as he pondered the warm bath, hearty meal and good night's sleep he'd enjoy when he got back home.

Right now, he could hear the team trudging up the mountain behind him, their voices lightly echoing through the gorge they were climbing. Jasmine set time with an old army marching song. Most joined in, but in between the beats, he could hear grumbling and cursing.

> "Supplies and morale were low too, but his instinct said they were close."

All of Jack's training told him they needed to stop, turn back and get home before the worst of the winter set in. He knew he was responsible for his troop, and they couldn't take much more. Yes, they'd been lucky, several cases of foot rot, one flesh wound to a buttock (strange) and one burst appendix. One of the creatives had surgical skills. Jack couldn't look, but Jasmine said it was a miracle, and he should be just as proud of his creatives as he was of his elite soldiers and those strange boys of his. He was, of course, but he didn't tell anyone. He didn't want to appear soft. Supplies and morale were low too, but his instinct said they were close. Yet he knew from reading the kingdom's history many had trod similar paths and failed, losing everything.

Jack stamped his feet, bringing life back to his frozen toes. He stepped forward. His right foot found solid ground, but

47

Leadership Magic

his left found nothing, and he tumbled head over heels through the air, landing with a soft thump into a snow drift. Snow went into his mouth, under his jacket, and up his trouser legs. His balaclava jammed down over his head, so when he stood up, he staggered around like a madman, thinking he had been blinded before realising the problem and wrenching the hat upwards. Above him, the troop arrived, the singing faltered to a stop, and he could see them looking left and right for him in the early evening gloom.

"Down here, you numbskulls," he yelled just before he slipped again, grabbing frantically at a spindly rowan tree with his right hand as a slab of ice moved under his feet. He turned and watched the snow slip down the mountain slope before dropping away into a blur of nothingness.

"Stay there, boss," yelled one of the soldiers, quickly hauling out a rope to make an anchor. Within minutes, Jack was back with them. Except now they had a problem. Jack hadn't accidentally slipped off the side of the track. He'd walked off the end. There was no more track; it had simply ended, vanished, except for a convenient ledge, one last stop before the slide, drop and likely avalanche down into the valley somewhere below them in the snow and mist. There was no way forward. All the team could see ahead were snowflakes and air. Jack tried to hold onto his disappointment, not express his crushing feeling of defeat. All around them were enclosing cliffs, outcrops and ice-covered rocks, with no way through – not even a sheep path. The gorge had taken them high and direct, and now there was only one way to go, and that was back.

Groundless Ground

Jack felt everyone's eyes looking, seeking his leadership reassurance. He went down on his haunches, a signal to huddle up for a briefing, except this time, there would be no brief. He had nothing to say. The team threw off their packs and either crouched down or made seats out of their kit, wanting a rest and a smoke. They knew the routine from their time together over the months. Every day, always a team talk. A straight honest conversation, where plans were made or changed, and then on they would go.

Jack took a deep breath. This was the worst moment of his career, one he never thought he would have to face. His team stared at him, trusting him, waiting for his words of calm which had seen them through so often.

"Sorry, everyone," he said so quietly that they had to lean forwards to hear him, his words coming out slowly, coated in the cold mist. "I think we have lost this one; it's all over. Time for the long walk home." He tried to keep his face calm and relaxed, but everyone saw the tear escape from his eye and roll down his cheek. Everyone looked at each other, dragged on cigarettes, pulled their scarves tighter and gloves higher. Anything other than look at Jack. Except for Isof, whispering madly to the other two strange ones. The troop were used to this. It was their normal behaviour, and they were odd, after all.

Then Isof spoke, "Cuse me, Gov, sorry, but you have got to be joking. This has to be the moment you have gone on and on about. All that useless training, stupid scenario planning, budgeting, rationing, yakety-yak. This is it!" He

49

Leadership Magic

would have said more, but his head had now disappeared inside his sack, which made everyone move nervously away from him. He popped out with a mega starburst firework in his hands. "You'll be needing this, the only way to see it," he said, winking at the other two strange ones, who nodded in agreement.

Jasmine, who had been slumped forward feeling exhausted, shot upwards off her pack. "Wait, he's right, this is it, this is it . . . groundless ground . . . this is the moment, we've found it," and she did a little hop and clicked her heels together.

"Groundless ground, groundless ground," the team mantra began and swelled up and around the team. The troop had practised it, talked about it, imagined it and listened to the King rant about it as they left, never really believing the moment would arrive. As they sang, stamping the rhythm on the icy ground with their boots, they watched Jack's head come up, and a broad smile appeared on his face.

> "They all saw it, a barely defined path through thin air, just two faint lines leading away from them."

The creatives were chattering madly, gesturing, pointing out into the mist. The soldiers looked confused; only Isof took action. He lit the starburst and hurled it out into the valley. The firework spiralled away from them, the touchpaper fizzing and turning in the semi-darkness before exploding, creating a broad arc of bright white light in front of them. They all saw it, a barely defined path through thin air, just two faint lines leading away from them. The firework dropped away, and the misty darkness closed in again. But everyone was left with the picture inside their mind and across their eyeballs.

"Okay," shouted Jack, all the exhaustion was gone, "let's go." He went to the end of the physical path and looked ahead. He could see it; he really could. He turned to Jasmine; she could see it too. Groundless ground – that mythical state before something new appears. Jack had grown up hearing these stories, hoping it was real, knowing you had to go over them to get to the future. He'd half-believed it, but here it was. He took a series of deep breaths and went inside to calm himself, to rehearse all the plans for this point, the attitude and the strength required. He also listened as his ancestors whispered good wishes into his ears.

> "The air held him, he seemed to walk on a solid nothingness, but as the others came behind, the path's shape appeared under their feet."

"Ready," Jack cried.

"Ready," the return cry came, bouncing back from the echoing mountain and his team.

"Another starburst, please, Isof." The firework flew upwards and exploded. Jack stepped forwards, his foot stepping into empty space. The air held him, he seemed to walk on a solid nothingness, but as the others came behind, the path's shape appeared under their feet. Then looking further back, a solid path was laid out behind them, which Isof, always last, was stamping on with his feet.

Jack knew what to do: look ahead, be confident, and hold the future in his head – and he did. Jasmine did too. He could sense her next to him, focusing and knowing how to walk on the groundless ground. Their team marched powerfully forwards in harmony too. Looking ahead, Jack could just make out some colour in the distance. Greens, yellows and distant music. Treasure awaited.

Finding a New Path – Utilising Your Unique Talents

Sometimes there comes a point when you know something has to change. No matter what you do, you are stuck, or you feel stuck. You know you have to step towards something different. Your present situation feels a little stagnant or just boring. Or it may be worse; the situation may be toxic and debilitating for you and those around you. A shift is needed.

The ability to "set off" and start out is key. A willingness to make a move, to take the first step, almost any move to get momentum for change. You may have a plan, a bit of a plan, or none at all. But start you must. Then often, things begin to shift around you. Perhaps you meet someone, you read something, or you simply find the second step. Hopefully, you discover different energy and ignite an interest in an area which is new and absorbing to you.

It isn't easy. We all need our familiar patterns, whether mental, emotional physical. Life with no regular familiar

Groundless Ground

ways can be exhausting. But those regular patterns can trap us into staying put, not changing. It is safe and secure to stay in one spot when we know we ought to move forwards when another part of us senses better opportunities elsewhere.

Groundless ground is a key concept in organisational or personal change. There is a real moment, a time when you have to move forwards. To follow and trust your plan. Yet there is a real sense of nothing solid to stand on, no tangible results, particularly in the early stages. Worse still, the sceptics (both your thoughts or inner feelings and real people around us) are waiting to complain about misuse of resources, poor management or the impact on the morale of these new, unproven ideas. Some people will talk of the need "to pull back", "stay in known markets", "stick with known products", and "not to take risks". This is a moment of leadership. The ability not just to stand on groundless ground but to walk forwards, taking others with you if they will come. Knowing the ground will form and become solid as you move ahead. Most of the sceptics will follow once the tarmac is laid, and there are a few streetlamps to show the way!

> "You may have a plan, a bit of a plan, or none at all. But start you must."

Prompts and Actions

Look around you. Are you in generally fertile lands, or do things need to change? Where do you need to trust yourself and move forward, and where might you need to risk a little?

Are you stuck in a specific situation? Are your wheels spinning in the mud somewhere? What resources do you need to begin moving forward? What is the first step?

Who do you need around you to break through to the next stage? Who will encourage you to move ahead? Who are your allies?

What can you do to support yourself and others when you are tired and want to give up? Who is your Jennie, your Isof? What mantras, songs and ways of working give you the energy to keep going?

When the moment comes to really step onto groundless ground, what will help you take that leap?

> *"The ultimate measure of yourself is not where you stand in moments of comfort and convenience, but where you stand at times of challenge and controversy."*
>
> ~ Martin Luther King Jr

CHAPTER FOUR
Power Surge

> You are powerful. Leadership positions are powerful. Understand your power; it has an impact and will make a difference. Learn how to calibrate this up and down as needed.

Nobody is speaking except the CEO, and she is raging. Barbara doesn't mean to attack, but she is demanding, straight-talking and has very high standards and expectations. The problem is that, rather than engaging her team, she seems to be driving them away.

I watch the various team members avoiding eye contact, making notes instead of engaging, and mumbling half-replies. I feel much the same as the coach and facilitator. At times Barbara is scary; her passion sometimes seems to verge on the edge of aggression. The mixture of her strong personality and strident style makes the business very successful. But at what price? I wonder as I watch the team stream rapidly from the weekly communications update.

Power Surge: Impact and Effectiveness

The clock ticked through to 2:30 p.m., and Molly wriggled in her seat. The spare chairs around the conference table in her office sat empty, the coffee and the water fresh, with ten cups and nine glasses neatly arranged. She sighed, drank her own water and stood up.

"Any sign of anyone, Jodie?" she called through to her PA as she checked her iPad for messages and emails.

"No, sorry. It all looks pretty busy out there," Jodie replied while squinting through the broad open-plan office. "To be fair, it is one of those days, and we have that major client in."

Molly knew that and understood the importance of this customer. She would be in the round-up, part of the sign-off later in the afternoon. Even so, she huffed and puffed to herself.

"Okay, no problem, but perhaps I'll take a stroll and see who I bump into," she said, setting off out of the executive suite and heading first to the Marketing department, where she intuitively felt more comfortable. It was her own original training, after all. Most of them were more extroverted and likely to keep a conversation going.

Fifteen minutes later, Molly's mood hadn't improved. People were polite and engaging. Some were clearly overwhelmed by having the CEO stop by their desks. Others were more interested in seeing her and chatting amiably about the business. No one, though, seemed able or willing to engage her in serious discussion. She knew he had a bit of an abrasive style and found social interactions a pain, so when the exec team suggested an open hour each week, it seemed like a great idea. Now she wasn't so sure. She wanted a fierce debate, challenge and honesty about the business and ideas for the future. Yes, the weekly open meeting and her conversations had been some of that, but more about pay, conditions, toilets, and the canteen. She was now seriously considering delegating the whole thing to HR. Then today, no one had turned up at all.

She stalked off through Operations and into Finance, asking questions and generally causing alarm and discomfort. She could see people slipping out from their desks and heading to the corridor, disappearing into the restrooms and creating queues at the coffee docks. Perhaps if one of her directors had been around, they could have bridged the gap, but all the senior management was tied up. So, after getting gruff one-word answers from the IT Analysts, she headed downstairs to the Facilities department. She had absolutely no interest in these things, but she'd heard about Jim, Head of Maintenance. He never came to any meeting whatsoever. Well, he should, and he would now, she thought. Maybe a one-to-one with the boss would wake him up a bit.

> "She wanted a fierce debate, challenge and honesty about the business and ideas for the future."

Leadership Magic

Molly banged her way through several safety doors, heading deeper into the bowels of the office. Past storerooms, skirting the central heating boiler room, past a desk, shoved up against the corridor wall, and finally into what looked like the main electrical source centre. Large leads snaked across the walls into boxes, each marked and colour coded. By a series of junction boxes, there lay on the floor two large leads waiting to be connected. Molly, ever inquisitive, went over to the large thick black cables, picked the two connectors up and looked carefully at the pins and sockets.

"Whoa there, mam, slow down, don't you be putting them together just yet," and a large gnarled, muscly hand appeared and took one wire away from her. "Just doing some work on that circuit, so best not plug it in right now. We're still running tests," said Jim, who knew exactly who Molly was and made no effort to treat her as the CEO.

Molly wasn't used to having things taken away and later wouldn't quite be able to recall why she did what she did next. Maybe frustration or just plain curiosity. Her parents always said it would get her into big trouble one day. Jim, when he told his mates in the pub later, chuckling over a beer, would call it "arrogance and stupidity" and say, "Yes, she did, she really did do it. She grabbed back the two connectors and rammed one into the other."

The room exploded into light, and a blue haze shot around them. Molly's feet lifted off the floor, her body vibrating and pulsing as the high-energy current coursed through her, pushing her hair up on end and making her eyes bulge in

Power Surge

their sockets. Jim, momentarily stunned by seeing his boss illuminated, shaking and seeming to gurgle slightly, leapt into action, launching himself across the room and slamming the main fuses off. Even without the power, Molly seemed to vibrate. Her hands gripped the connectors with her fingers clamped rigidly around the plastic fittings. Jim prised her fingers free and guided her to a chair.

"Steady boss, steady, that was a real bolter you just took there. Just sit for a moment. Do you need me to get the first aider down?"

Molly sucked in big lungfuls of air, ran her fingers through her upright hair, closed her eyes and then laughed. "Now that's what I call power, real power. You feel it right in your heart," and she thumped her chest. "Power really does vibrate. Woohoo, give me more."

> "Now that's what I call power, real power. You feel it right in your heart."

"Geez, you're one crazy nutcase," Jim said, "who really enjoys being almost killed?"

"It isn't that; it's just real. That's what power is," Molly sucked in more air. "Jim, honestly, that's what it's like in my job, but it's difficult to describe, and I've just experienced it. Physically experienced it," and again, she touched her chest. "Power at my level is just like that, and if you don't take care, it is dangerous, yet fun, fun, fun."

"Yeah, right and abusive too," retorted Jim, not afraid to answer back. "Some of you are just plain bullies, throwing your weight around." Including you, he thought to himself.

Leadership Magic

"Yes, including me. I need to learn how to stop jumping in and bossing people about. And see, I'm pretty good at guessing what you are thinking, so just say it from now on; tell it to me straight."

Jim nodded, then shook his head, laughed, reached into his lunch bag and pulled out his coffee flask. He added two large sugars to both drinks and watched Molly uncurl her fingers, crack her knuckles, take the coffee and swallow it in two large gulps.

Jim sensing the opportunity, leant over and eyeballed his boss, which was tricky as one pupil was massively dilated while the other had shrunk to a pinprick of blackness.

"You know you could take more of us with you if you just thought about the power you and the executives have. I'm used to electrical power, you felt it just know, it's strong stuff. Down here, we need to be professional, assess the risks and manage them well. I reckon management power is similar. Not to be abused or used to mistreat people, but really important to get things done. Maybe just take care of how you use it." He leaned back in his chair, taking a slurp of his coffee, waiting for her reply.

> "There's nothing so grand as a story about the boss, and this one whipped around the building. The meeting room was packed at the next open hour."

"Well maybe, hum well, let me think," muttered Molly staring back, her eyes gradually normalising and returning to their usual green, brown colour. She pulled herself out of the chair, put down her cup, shook Jim's hand and, with a slight stagger, left the basement.

There's nothing so grand as a story about the boss, and this one whipped around the building. The meeting room was packed at the next open hour. Even Jim was there. The conversation was varied, relaxed at times, almost soft and sometimes spiky and demanding. Molly mostly listened, interjecting occasionally and, in the quieter moments, reflected on power and how a shock occasionally was a good wake-up call.

Personal Power and Authority
– Using Power Wisely

Most of us know someone who seems to exude power and confidence. These people have a natural way of taking control of just about any situation. It's part of their natural way of working. We all have personal power, but some of us can only access it in particular circumstances, maybe when emotions are high, or we are in a difficult situation. If we arrive at leadership positions, some handle this authority and the need to exercise power well. Others struggle to regulate this – too high, too low – or worse, some misuse this position of responsibility, abusing power entrusted to them. Ego begins to take over. Ego is

"We need self-understanding to manage our ego and power carefully."

Leadership Magic

important to live our lives well, to push us forward, and to ensure we are not swamped and taken advantage of by others. Yet we need self-understanding to manage our ego and power carefully. We have all met people who do this well, the compassionate, caring manager and its opposite, the malevolent dictator whose power appears to corrupt and damage those around them.

The most interesting thing is when we all use our personal power wisely, amazing things happen. And isn't it enjoyable to be in successful situations where everyone uses their power to serve the greater good?

Prompts and Actions

How flexible are you with your personal or positional power? Do you have more than one management style? Can you flex depending on the situation? Can you calibrate your power?

As a person, particularly if you lead others, are you aware of your impact? Where is this impact positive, and where is it negative? Does anything need to change? Who is willing to give you feedback on your power and influence?

Right now, where do you need to use your power more, less, or differently? How could you do this? What might the impact of that be for yourself, others around you, your organisation, and the local community?

CHAPTER FIVE
James Goes Running

> Find and use all the resources around you. If you are stuck, stop, reshape and then move on again. Find ways to re-energise yourself. Do something different and find what works for you.

William sits opposite, trying to smile, telling me of his hopes, but sadness seems to come across the room and beat his outer optimism. He hasn't been in work for six months, and he tells me he can't find the right position. He wants something new, but nothing compares to his job, the one he was made redundant from. He tells me this is the ideal time in his career to make a change and have a fresh start. He's diligent and works hard at job hunting. His approach is sound, and his standards are high. He's applying for jobs but often doesn't hear back after putting hours into individual applications. He's tired, depressed, deflated and lacks any energy.

James Goes Running: Being Resourceful

James pulled out the dusty mud-crusted running shoes from the bag he'd thrown them into all that time ago. Down here in the cellar, all was quiet, just the occasional hiss of the boiler as it began heating the house for the day ahead. He sat on the steps and pulled on each shoe, tightening the laces to just the right tension, ready for the road ahead.

With a deep breath and pulling back his shoulders, he took the steps two at a time, the running shoes creaking as he moved to leave dried earth behind on the steps. Out of the house, he walked to the gate, turned onto the road and set off at a gentle pace, shaking the sleepiness from his joints and muscles. He took a deep breath, reminded of what a great time of day it was before everyone woke up. The calmness and tranquillity, no noise yet from the houses as he padded gently past.

Before long, James was in a rhythm, his body remembering and adjusting to the style and pace he ran. His breathing regulated and steadied. Now his mind dropped into neutral, and he began to notice the world around him, moving from outer attention and inwards, mulling and considering the day ahead and beyond that, his future and a new job. The birds chattered, another runner passed with a cheery hello, and a smart BMW roared by as the "bright young thing" from next door shot past on his way to catch the 6.30 a.m. commuter train to London. He took the slight hill ahead easily and confidently, letting his legs stretch out and enjoy themselves.

James Goes Running

"Morning James, good to be out and about, hey? Lovely time of day for a run, I say," and James looking to his left, found he was running next to a rather rotund man with billowing shorts that came down to his knees, bright yellow trainers and a blue basketball hat crammed down over a bush of bright ginger curly hair. He ran with unerring confidence and strength, considering his size and shape. He thrust out his hand.

"CC's my name, Captain Confidence, but most people abbreviate it. We all need to believe in ourselves, James. I'm your man to help there," he said, nudging James in the ribs, his elbow seeming to send shock waves into James's chest and directly up to his brain, where a fizz and a pop suddenly made the world a bit brighter and sharper, the birds now chirruping loudly in his ears.

> "A fizz and a pop suddenly made the world a bit brighter and sharper, the birds now chirruping loudly in his ears."

CC settled into a steady rhythm next to him and whistled as they turned left into the park and set off around the perimeter track.

"Morning CC, morning James, good to see you both." James, startled, moved his eyes away from CC to his left and saw a tall, gangly runner next to him wearing a trilby hat and a long overcoat, neither of which impeded his movement. His height meant he seemed to walk rather than run and strode next to them.

"Reginald Resourcefulness here. Good to make your acquaintance. Now, what do you need?" He said, pulling

Leadership Magic

open his coat to reveal pockets stuffed with everything you could imagine.

"Maybe a map, or a compass, perhaps some Kendal Mint Cake, or better still, a brand-new pair of running shoes." With a broad flourish, he dived into an inside pocket and revealed a pair of the latest Nikes.

"Later, later, old chap," retorted CC. "Plenty of time for all that. Let's just get into a good steady rhythm first," and the three of them set off along the path together.

> "He felt carried along and somehow supported by them."

"You'll definitely need contacts. I have a whole book full here," whispered Reggie to James, showing him surreptitiously a small leather-bound notepad before sliding it back into his pocket. James smiled. He thought his first run would be hard, yet it wasn't, not physically or mentally. Running between the two, he felt carried along and somehow supported by them.

Together they swept round the bottom corner of the park and headed toward the bandstand. To everyone's surprise, the local town band sat tuning up, just as though it was a summer Sunday afternoon. The bandmaster seeing them, lifted his baton, the band struck up, and music flowed towards them, almost lifting them off their feet with its depth and resonance. The notes fell and rose in time with their running, and the instruments seemed to share in their journey, from the big bass drum with its steady regular deep beat to the tiny piccolo picking out softer detail. James's

James Goes Running

heart lifted, and a broad smile came to his face. He felt his toes lift his feet, and his stride grew until he almost flew off the floor. CC, Reggie and James glided past the town band on and around the side of the park.

With a mistimed note on the E flat tuba and a clash of the cymbals, the music came to a sudden halt as the bandmaster leapt from the stand and rushed after the three runners, waving his baton madly.

"Wait, wait . . . wait for us," and he beckoned behind for the band to follow him. "Don't you want inspiring music to help you along?"

"Sounds great to me," said Reggie, ever resourceful and thinking of other places this band might come in useful. CC didn't reply. He was still bobbing about and singing to the last tune. He skipped lightly over the grass, jumping up on the park benches, seeming to float, and then landing perfectly on the ground. James liked the band; the sound inspired his running. Without thinking of the consequences, he invited the band to go on the adventure with them. So off they went. James, Reggie and CC took longer and longer steps and found, with the music playing, they could hurdle the park benches easily, gliding effortlessly through the air.

"He felt his toes lift his feet, and his stride grew until he almost flew off the floor."

The band, not quite as fit or able, tried to keep up but lacked the puff to run and play simultaneously. So, being crafty – and as the three went around the park's perimeter –

Leadership Magic

they cut across the grass, saving time and energy. Allowing the trumpet players to have a quick smoke, too, while they waited for the three runners to arrive.

James returned to the park gate after several circuits and turned into the street. The music faded, and looking back, he saw the band waving him off. And leaning against the metal railings stood CC and Reggie. "We're around any time, for sure, anytime you're out running, but other times too. Just let us know, and we'll get our running shoes ready." Both gently saluted him as he sped away down the street.

At home, James stopped and did some gentle stretches to finish his run. He felt calm and relaxed, ready to face the day. Not bad for a first-time out in ages, he thought. A good pace. His muscles ached slightly from the workout. And clicking through his mind were all sorts of ideas for developing his career. He marched up the garden path, humming a catchy tune he'd heard earlier and headed in for a shower . . . work called.

Being Resourceful – Asking for and Receiving Help, Staying Motivated

It has always amazed me how people sometimes seem stuck, lacking motivation, and unable to access resources and help. Then, after thinking it through, they – nine times out of ten – can come up with ways to resolve the issue. What appears to happen is the willingness to face the issue directly; facing the key questions creates a new strength and determination.

James Goes Running

Energy appears, and new creativity creates more options and possibilities going forward.

So, if you have a problem, get motivated and do something. Experiment with something new. And if you can't get motivated . . . when it seems easier to sit with the pain, the sluggishness, the disappointment of it all . . . then get your body moving! Get up, go for a walk, do some exercise, put on loud music and maybe dance.

"Momentum matters. Just a little resourcefulness, some small movement attracts more movement."

And guess what? As your heart stirs, blood moves through your body, oxygen moves to the brain, which begins to slurp, swish and slop, and new thoughts begin!

When you are moving, you can increase this effect by getting more people around you. Not to dump your problem on them (even if that feels good at the time), but to get new perspectives, more ideas and different suggestions. We all think; differently. We all have a wealth of life experiences. One of those new perspectives might be just the lever to shift that rock in front of you. So, share your questions with others; they want to help.

But (isn't there always a but!) you have to want to do this. The start is your start, not someone else's. Taking a new direction isn't always that easy. When it feels tough, it probably is. So, sometimes just accept that and sit with your problem for a while. Then move on, take the next step forward, and even if you slip back, keep moving. Momentum matters. Just a

Leadership Magic

little resourcefulness, some small movement attracts more movement. And celebrate small steps, the progress you've made, even if tiny. Record and verbalise success to build your positivity. Watch your flywheel begin to spin and create the results you want.

P.S. William got the job he wanted; he persevered and got there.

Prompts and Actions

Imagine you need to shift something in your business, in yourself. Or maybe you are looking to make a career move too:

Do you know the resources you have available that are within you? Can you list and verbalise them? Are there other resources you sense you need? Can you articulate these? Are there people who you need to contact to ask for their help and guidance?

How confident are you? Is your confidence grounded in reality? Can you sense it and feel its natural strength? Can you describe your individual skills and talents well? How can you use your confidence to help you?

Are you fit enough for the journey ahead, physically, mentally and emotionally? How do you maintain high performance to move ahead daily to achieve your plans? If you're stuck, what do you need to unblock yourself and make that first step?

What inspires you and keeps you going when work, or life in general, may be tough? Is it listening to music, looking at wonderful art, being outdoors or reading great books? Where do you go to lift yourself up and find a different or creative direction?

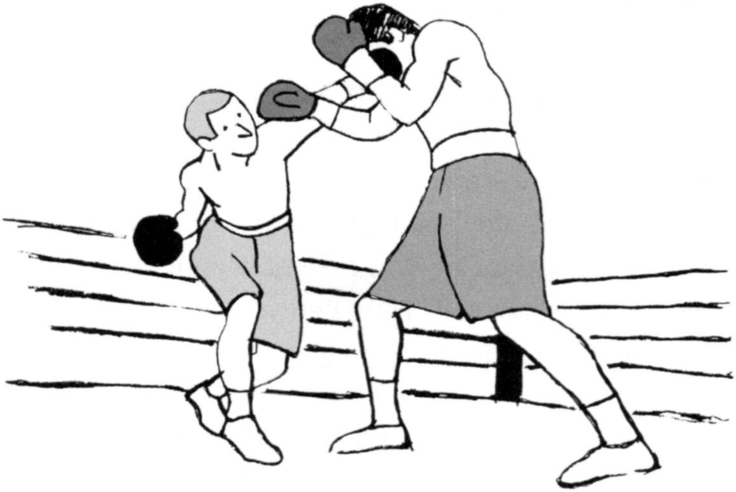

CHAPTER SIX
Knockout Fight

> Focus on your talent and understand the gifts you have. Be willing to put the time in to develop your skills. Listen to feedback, shift and change but trust yourself. You know what you do best.

Joe has skill, real talent, honing this with dedicated attention. As a musician, he is just wonderful to listen to. He has worked hard, doing courses to develop his voice and instrumental skills and taking all sorts of musical and support act jobs to put himself in front of people. He is writing his own songs, marketing them, and covering every base as a music entrepreneur. I can see and hear, as he describes his daily work, the effort that he has put into his career. He won't give up, I'm sure of that. But it is a tough profession, full of creativity which needs lots of self-discipline and application. He sits on the sofa in our lounge, and I help him plan the next steps and the focus he will need.

Knockout Fight: Self-Belief

"In the left-hand corner representing joy, hope, anticipation, creativity, please give it up for Santosh, our latest contender for the world title," the announcer's voice booms around in the darkness, followed by muted clapping from the auditorium. Santosh waves and, after a tentative half-confident walk around the ring, settles on his stool in the corner. As his gloves are tightened, he listens to his coaching team go through the final briefing.

"Come on, Santosh, you can do it," calls a lone voice, making him smile. His mum is in the crowd, willing him on, as she has at every bout since he'd chosen to take up boxing. Now she's up on her feet chanting his name, and others are half-heartedly joining in. It doesn't matter one way or another to her. She's there for her son and will be forever. Now she's turning round, shouting up into the rows behind. That gets the boozed-up ones going, jeering, catcalling, telling her to "Fuck off, sit down." The PA system booms into life, drowning the argument. Then the lights are flashing, followed by billowing iced smoke, which swirls around the long corridor from the changing rooms to the ring.

"And now, ladies and gentlemen, please welcome the defending and heavyweight champion of the world, representing doubt, worry, failure, despondency, Mr DWFD, or, as we know him, Baaaaad Boooooy."

The crowd are on their feet, stamping to the music, clapping and shouting. Emerging out of the smoke is the biggest opponent Santosh has ever seen. He fills the space, not just

Knockout Fight

physically but emotionally and mentally too. He's huge and threatening and ignores the crowd as he strides to the ring, squeezing through the ropes and eyeballing Santosh with a sarcastic, arrogant look. The commentator reels off the belts and titles that Bad Boy has won. The crowds howl their delight, and everyone can feel the anticipation of another annihilation ahead. It reminds Santosh of a fox hunt, a bloodletting. The closest people can come to war without getting hurt themselves. Baying for damage and destruction. Santosh's mum does her best, shouting back and waving her arms until a steward physically pushes her down into her chair and holds her there as she screams at him.

Bad Boy begins his ritual, pacing around the ring, beating his chest and growling. Coming closer to Santosh's corner every time before finally walking right up to him and spitting on the floor between his legs. Santosh looks at the globule of phlegm and laughs, not caught by the drama, then he stands, screws his boot symbolically into the spit and raises his gloves.

> "Take the game to the opponent, don't let him get into a groove, and keep him guessing."

The bell hasn't rung, and the referee is about to give the normal set-piece lecture, but it's too late; they're off. Santosh is dancing around the ring, skipping to the music, which suddenly stops as the management realises what's happening. Bad Boy isn't happy. He's used to dominating from the word go. He growls a "fuck you," lumbers towards Santosh and swings an arm. The right cut slices through the air; he's fast, and he knows it. The silence in the crowd says they know it too and suspect it'll all be over before the bell has even rung. Not Santosh, though. He ducks and pivots, the boxing glove hissing past his face making Bad Boy stumble as he boxes into empty space.

Santosh's mum is on her feet again, yelling. The neutrals in the crowd are suddenly shouting for Santosh, and new bets are placed. Santosh's heart is bounding. He's following the drill the team has agreed to. Take the game to the opponent, don't let him get into a groove, and keep him guessing. Right, thinks Santosh, great theory, but this guy is huge, deadly, and now he's mad too. The sweat begins to trickle down his face as he dances away and around the ring, making Bad Boy chase him. He neatly ducks away as his opponent tries to trap him in the corner, even getting a soft punch to the Bad Boy's arm before skipping away again.

One minute, two minutes, he's still there skipping, weaving, occasionally making a punch but largely staying out of trouble, following the game plan for round one, just a few seconds more. On your toes, stay focused. That is the mantra, and his last thought as the pile driver hits him – the glove smacking into his face, the soft leather crumbling against his cheek before fully making contact, lifting Santosh off his feet and throwing him across the ring. He sees the crowd, the lights, and, from the corner of his eye, his mum gasping with her hands to her mouth in horror. There isn't much more before his head hits the floor, and he's out cold.

"Five-uh, six-uh," Santosh can hear the count through the

Knockout Fight

haze. He knows he has to get up but can't. Everything has gone to mush. His corner is yelling; he hears them. "Seven-uh, eight-uh." It's all over. He can't get up. Then he's on his knees, and blood drips from his nose onto the canvas. "Nine-uh." He's on his feet, just bent over but up. Bad Boy snarls and charges him; the bell rings, and the referee tries to intervene, but Bad Boy has none of it and brushes him aside before smacking Santosh on the nose and crashing him back onto the ropes.

There is an uproar. The crowd want a fight, but a relatively fair one. Santosh's mum is climbing into the ring and being pulled back by the radio commentator whose microphone she has just sent flying as she stands on his crib notes. Santosh is a crumbled heap on the floor. He looks dead, and his team gather on their knees around him. The smelling salts are waved under his nose. The referee mutters about stopping the fight. The competition doctor is being summoned. It looks like it's all over, and Bad Boy has done it again.

Santosh remembers getting to his feet, seeing the red stain on the canvas, and then hearing the sound of his nose breaking, but nothing else. Now he thinks he can hear people talking, a face with a bowtie peering at him, looking into each of his eyes, and then he slips away.

"Woah there, boy, where are you going?" Santosh wakes to find himself walking past a gardener digging a vegetable patch, who is now leaning on his spade and eyeing him up and down. His eyes sparkle under his weather-beaten cap. Santosh can see the path he's on stretching off into the distance and turns to go.

Leadership Magic

"Funny gear to be wearing for a walk, if you don't mind me saying," and he points a dirty finger at Santosh's bright blue shorts and the boxing gloves on his hands.

"Um, yeah, well, you know. Well, never mind, I've got to be going now." His eyes are drawn to the road ahead, which looks warm and inviting, with the sun glinting in the distance.

"Ah ha, okay, but do you want some advice?"

Santosh doesn't want to hear this old boy's thoughts. He just feels like a right idiot standing here half-dressed, and he waves his gloves around in a circle trying to be polite and, without realising it, did a little jink and circle as though he was sparring in the practice gym.

"Classy, real style. If I didn't know better, I'd say that's natural talent I'm looking at there." The gardener rams his spade into the soil and moves over towards Santosh. "I have plenty of people pass me here, you know. Most don't even see me; they're just busy rushing by." He turns to look at the sun in the distance, and it plays onto his wrinkled face creating shadows and highlights.

"You know they've had a go at something – given it their best shot, hit some failure. I guess that might have happened to you, hey?" He winked and pointed at the soft gloves on Santosh's hands. "I don't judge because using your talent, well, that isn't easy. I know everyone who comes past here has given it a good go. Others don't even start, so well done you, but I wonder . . ." and the gardener seemed to drift away into his thoughts before turning, picking a large ripe tomato and fitting it neatly into the palm of Santosh's right-hand glove. "Known to have superpowers, these tomatoes, you know. Me, I don't know, but they taste great with a bit of salad. Enjoy."

So Santosh does, but it's tricky. It's not just holding the tomato in a boxing glove but eating it, too, because it slips and slides and bursts as he bites into it. The taste is exquisite and fills him with warm, hopeful sensations as he swallows.

"Come on, Santosh, let's go," the shock of the water on his face and a towel roughly rubbed over his nose, coming away red and snotty, brings him around. Then the bell rings, and he's back on his feet. Wobbly, yes, and nervous, but he's ready to fight again. He tastes tomato in his mouth. Have his backup team been feeding him supplements between rounds? He can't remember. He can, though, hear the crowd rooting for him now and booing as Bad Boy comes lumbering towards him, leering and cursing. Santosh thinks his team must have given him some drugs because he can feel his energy returning. And then he's back on his toes, dancing a little, bruised but already thinking through a new plan. Audaciously he waves to the crowd. They roar back, and he feels their support. He notices his mum standing on the press table, howling too. The commentators are going mad, not at his mother; they've given up trying to control her. Now they are peering around her legs up to the ring, shouting into microphones. They sense a shock is on the cards, and it is.

Santosh wipes his nose with the back of his glove, then

spits on the floor and quietly says to himself, "You can do this, you've trained, you're good, you've done this on a smaller scale before, but you've got to fight and fight smart." Then he's away parrying, jabbing, bouncing in and out of range. His team yells instructions, the gym work comes back, the practice moves, the tactics of previous fights. He can see it all in his mind, and then he sees the final move.

Bad Boy is worried now. He's run out of ideas and finds himself chasing Santosh around the ring, hoping to trap him in a corner. He doesn't see it coming. A shimmy, a duck, a punch to the stomach, making him double up. Then the hook to his chin, and he topples backwards like a large tree.

> "He can see it all in his mind, and then he sees the final move."

"Timber!" shouts a smart Alec in the crowd, and time seems to stand still until the torso of Bad Boy hits the canvas with a resounding thud. Santosh doesn't look. His right hand hurts too much. It must be broken. He can't go on. The pain is shooting up his arm and into his shoulder. He wants to sit down, lie down, anything to take away the shock, but he hears his team telling him to stay there and walk, and in a daze, he listens to the count. The auditorium erupts. He's done it. He's knocked out Bad Boy.

Santosh doesn't usually dream; he's usually just exhausted at the end of the day. Yet tonight, he does. He's wearing his winner's belt, and he's back with the gardener, and they are both laughing and recreating the fight in the garden.

Knockout Fight

Santosh pretends to knock out the old man, which he does carefully as his wrist and arm are plastered up to the elbow. The gardener falls gently backwards amongst the rows of vegetables and flowers, squashing the carrots and giggling to himself before pointing up at Santosh and saying, "Yup, that's some talent you've got there. Watch out, world!"

Talent – Finding and Using It and Not Giving Up

We all have a talent. I really believe that. For some people, this is obvious, and we can all see what they do well and how they make their talent appear in the world. For others, it is harder to spot our uniqueness and the difference we bring. It seems hidden. Or worse still, our talent has somehow been beaten out of us by well-intentioned people who tell us, "That's not possible," "Be realistic," or "Wake up; life's not a dream, you know."

Talent can be frustrating too. It seems to shift and move across a lifetime, appearing, disappearing.

> "Talent can be frustrating too. It seems to shift and move across a lifetime, appearing, disappearing."

What is it? Where is it? Was it something I was born with, a natural skill? Or is it something I find along the way, something to be developed?

For some of us, talent can be something large and obvious

Leadership Magic

– we are "good at art" or "great with numbers", and opportunities come to us quite easily. For others, it is more elusive and appears as something smaller, yet when applied may have a huge impact. A CEO who is very successful told me his true talent was recruiting and developing other key leaders. This wasn't obvious when he was younger (he chased the numbers), but the teams he puts together now have a massive impact on the world and produce great results.

You may have to fight for your talent, though. Put the time in, nurture and grow it. You may need to go on courses, test ideas out and experiment, but it will grow and expand as you put the time in. And if you don't, the opposite is true; it may wither and disappear. Similarly, don't expect others to see or respect your talent. Often, a powerful talent unnerves other people or creates a competitive reaction.

> "You may have to fight for your talent, though. Put the time in, nurture and grow it."

So, find and develop your talent. Don't give up on it, even when you are unsure or can't take it forward (some talents won't make money, there doesn't seem to be a direct correlation between a talent and a career). Look for people who can help you, who understand the concept, and who won't let you sell yourself short. Mix with those who root for you and are not afraid to offer you direct, honest feedback and guidance to accelerate your development.

Prompts and Actions

Do you know your talent(s)? Are you using them well, honouring the skills you have been given?

Are there blocks to using your talent? What can you do about them?

Who can support, help you, encourage and challenge you to keep moving forward, perhaps point out a new direction or how to address an issue differently?

On the other side, who do you know that deserves your support and encouragement? Maybe someone younger, a friend needing to make a change, a member of your family?

At work, how are talented people supported? Are you pushing individuals to work well and productively every day? How much talent does your team have? Could these be used more?

Out in the world, what can you and I do, with the talents we have, to help tilt the world to a safer, stronger place?

CHAPTER SEVEN

Something's Moving in the Garden

> Expect challenges, bias and misunderstanding when building something new. People may want this new future, but not always the change involved to get there.

Jo is angry. She looks at me in frustration, telling me it shouldn't be this hard to develop a smaller, embryonic, entrepreneurial business within the structure of the larger organisation she works in. Why is it such a struggle? I wonder. Everyone wants her business to be successful. However, the shape and direction she is taking are so different from the core organisation that most people struggle to get their heads around the concept, let alone the practicalities. And then there is a whole group of people who are jealous of her ideas and her freedom to experiment, even though she still has to deliver

Leadership Magic

results, turnover and profit the same way as everyone else.

We talk about difference and diversity, chatting about a metaphor when a strange mystical creature appears, disturbing all that has gone before.

Something's Moving in the Garden: Difference and Diversity

"Daddy, Daddy, there's something in the flowerpot. Come look, please come and look." Her face radiates towards me, the blond curls spilling out under her bright red bobble hat. Her gloves dangle by their strings out of her coat, and I see her muddy hands just a second before she grabs my trouser leg to get me out of my chair.

"Woo, steady, I'm coming." I fold up my newspaper and try to forget the quiet ten minutes I was having. We head out through the patio doors into the cold winter air, and I immediately realise I should have put on a coat. Sue, my wife, is down in the garden digging a flowerbed, throwing weeds behind her. I resist the desire to call out and remind her this was my time, and we'd agreed she and Lucy would garden together.

"Come on, Daddy, hurry up – this way," Lucy, our smart, insistent daughter, says, trotting ahead of me. I feel a glow of pride watching her young confidence and remember the nativity play at school the week before. She was an angel and a junior one at that, with just three words to speak – "Peace and joy." The hot, stuffy hall full of cameras and phones

Something's Moving in the Garden

flashing. A confusing Christmas story full of sharks, zebras, a London post-box, six kings and our daughter. There she is . . . I see her vividly in her angel dress, her lines delivered slowly with loud perfection, each we'd practised every night before bed after storytime. My heart swells at the memory. I just know she'll be on the stage one day.

"Look here, look." I peer into an extra-large plastic flowerpot sitting on the floor of our small greenhouse amongst the dry, dusty bean canes. It's the pot I had every intention of putting the Christmas tree in later, once I'd finished the sports pages. A strange animal looks up at me. A long snout, two large nostrils, a broad crinkled back and an even bigger tail, which swishes and cracks against the pot sides, making the whole thing jump and vibrate. The eyes dare me to come forward, and I am tempted to put my hands into the pot and then change my mind.

> "A strange animal looks up at me. A long snout, two large nostrils, a broad crinkled back and an even bigger tail."

"Isn't it sweet, Daddy? Can we keep it, please, Daddy, please?" Lucy jumps up and down on the spot, hopping from one leg to the other with excitement. Then her voice changes. "There, there, calm down, little one." I hear Lucy recite her mother's words with the same intonation and softness and the thing settles, curling up, no longer banging the pot across the greenhouse floor. Before I can stop her, Lucy puts her grubby fingers in and rubs the top of its nose, calming it even more. There is a strange purring sort of noise.

"I wouldn't do that, Lucy, just in case, you know. Well, it might have teeth," and I tug at her coat and pull her away.

"No, no, Daddy, he likes being picked up and cuddled. Look . . ." and she scoops the alligator-looking reptile up in her arms. It flops over her shoulder like a ragdoll, snout hanging down her back, steam puffing out of its nostrils into the cold garden air. "He's a bit too heavy, though. Can you take him?"

I carefully take the reptile from Lucy, unpeeling his claws that are sticking in her woolly coat. My hands pass around the rough, scaly body, and I gently but firmly put him back in the pot. He doesn't fit anymore and now drapes half in and half out.

"Wow, he's grown," Sue says, dumping a load of weeds on the compost and joining us in the greenhouse. Together we watch the creature settle down, tail and rear end in the pot, the rest slumped over on the ground. First, one eye closes, then another. The purring changes to a gentle snore.

"Lucy showed me earlier; it looked like a lizard then – now I'm not so sure. Maybe it's escaped from a pet shop or something," said Sue. That had been exactly my thought, but there wasn't one near us, so my mind went to the beatnik guy who lives three doors down. He had a snake once, but that was before we had Lucy. Then when he settled down with that new girlfriend, the posh one, I'm pretty sure he got a dog instead.

"I could ask that snake guy at number twenty, or maybe we just phone the RSPCA," I say.

Something's Moving in the Garden

Lucy looks up at me, and I explain the charity that helps sick and lost animals. She nods wisely and, tilting her head to look at me, says, "but we will be able to keep him, won't we? It would be the best Christmas present ever. Please."

Sue and I look at each other.

"Tell you what, let's have lunch, a boiled egg with soldiers, and we'll decide afterwards. How about that?" I swing her onto my shoulders and stride up the garden path, away from what seems like a complicated problem.

"Right mate, what you got then? A baby crocodile, the call said. Seems unlikely, but we get all sorts of things to deal with, you know." He's standing on the doorstep, his RSPCA uniform not quite fitting, like he's outgrown it. A beer belly hangs over his belt. He looks competent, though, if a bit rough around the edges.

"Okay, I've got a cat travel cage here, and if it's bigger, this noose will hold it while we deal with it. This sorts out wild dogs, so it should do the job." I look at the cage and then the pole with a rope circle and decide not to engage in a conversation. I'm not sure either will do, but it's getting dark, so I show him through the house into the garden. Two pinpricks of light come from the greenhouse, and the purring has turned to a low rumble.

"Right, let's be having you," and flicking on his torch, the man strides forward across the lawn.

The blast of heat and flame shocks us all. Two small jets, like a pair of blowtorches, arc towards us, smacking against the RSPCA man's boots, charring the laces.

Leadership Magic

"Fireworks, Mummy!" shrieks Lucy with joy, wriggling to get away from Sue's hand, which is holding her tightly. No one can believe it, but it doesn't matter because the greenhouse has begun to shake. One by one, with a bang, each pane shatters, sending slivers of glass spinning into the night. The frame begins to twist and buckle. Then crashing out of one end is a head, and at the other, a tail, flicking and crashing against the fence. With one last pop, the frame disintegrates, aluminium pings everywhere and there standing in front of us . . .

"A dragon, Daddy, a dragon, just like those pictures in the book. Mummy, Mummy, Father Christmas has brought us a dragon, a real dragon." Lucy is jumping up and down. My mouth is open. Sue backs away, and the RSPCA man drops his alligator noose and runs. The dragon sits back on his haunches and, with a soft thud, settles down on top of the vegetable patch, his tail moving back and forth. Then it seems to wink at us.

My Brussels, my Christmas spuds, the turnips are all I can think of as the dragon slumps forward, his head crashing down on the patio. He looks lovingly up at us. Warm air from his nose blows across our legs, and with a contented sigh, he drops off to sleep again.

After a sleepless night, we are no further forward. We're sitting in the dining room, looking out into the garden.

"I don't know what to do. Stop asking," I say. We've been around the subject endless times as we watch the dragon through the steamed-up glass door.

Something's Moving in the Garden

"Well, he doesn't seem to have grown overnight, so that's a relief. And are you sure it's a he? It may be a she. In fact, I'm sure it's a she." Sue looks at me over her coffee cup as we watch Lucy outside, leaning against the dragon and patting his skin gently.

"This is either very dangerous, in which case I should rescue my daughter, or I am in the middle of a very strange dream. Perhaps I'll wake up soon?" I shake my head, but nothing changes. Inside, I have an amazing sense of calm, which is crazy, given the situation.

Looking up, I see Lucy, "Don't grab . . ."

Too late, Lucy is gently pulling at the dragon's eyelashes, intrigued by their length and colour. The dragon doesn't seem put out at all and closes both eyes to let her run fingers through and across the coarse black fibres, like running fingers across a piano keyboard.

"Now we're late, got to dash. I'm sure you'll sort this out before we're back." With a peck on Sue's cheek, I grab my bag and head out.

"Come on, Lucy, time to go. Remember it's dad's and daughter's day, then the party later." We have this wonderful tradition where on the last day before Christmas, children are invited into the office, and we finish with a kids' party at lunchtime. This is the first year for Lucy. She gives the dragon a kiss and skips over to me. We head to the car.

There's a thud as I clip Lucy into her seat. The car rocks slightly then I feel a breath on my shoulder.

"No, no, get out, you beast!" But it's too late; the dragon

Leadership Magic

is squashed in the back of the car, his head resting between the front seats and immediately the temperature rises, and we're in the tropics. The frozen windscreen clears instantly, and the rubber seal around the edge begins to overheat and smell. I am about to complain, then notice the curling lip and a large set of sharp white teeth emerging. And above, a slow lazy wink of an eye. I carefully and apologetically push the snout to one side, find the gear stick under the folds of rough skin and set off.

"Morning. You must be Lucy, and you've brought your dinosaur too. Well done, just sign here." The security officer at reception leans forward and smiles. I lift Lucy and hold her as she slowly writes her name across the visitor's pad in large capital letters.

"It's amazing what they can do now, isn't it? Looks just like the real thing too." The security man stares at the dragon. "And it even smells. What'll they think of next, hey? Look, it winks. Now that's smart. Pricey, I imagine. Do they do a smaller version at all? Sold out probably by now. Toy of the year, is it? Maybe I can get one in the sales in January . . ." He chatters on. He always does. I nod mostly in the mornings; it nearly always seems too early for chatty conversation. Lucy hands him the pen, and the security man looks at her name, covering twenty of the official visitor signature boxes on the form.

"Right, okay, guys, let's go," and the three of us squashed into the elevator. I can't help smiling as we step in. We practise counting the numbers on the panel, with the

Something's Moving in the Garden

dragon thumping its tail on the floor when Lucy hits ten. The elevator is still bouncing up and down as the door slides open on my floor.

Some people look. Others don't even notice as we walk through the open-plan office. At my desk, Lucy points at the family photos beside my overflowing in-tray, able to name each person, touching her fingers to the glass. The dragon comes close and examines each one, seeming to nod approval. As he moves, he inadvertently knocks files and expense reports onto the floor and then swishes them into a muddle with his feet and tail.

"CEO needs you in the boardroom now, some sort of emergency." Jane floats into the room, all competence and smartness. She is organised to the hilt, keeps the executive team on track, and is the best assistant I have worked with.

"Hi, Lucy, why don't you come with me for a few minutes? I've heard all about you. Daddy has a meeting to go to." She doesn't even notice the dragon, who begins to hiss as Lucy bursts into tears and hides behind my legs. I watch Jane move back towards her desk as I tell her, "I'll deal with this and that. Sorry, Lucy isn't good with strangers."

"Are you sure? Oh, all right."

The CEO is muttering, unsure how to handle a child in the boardroom. But Lucy is quietly sitting on my lap, tucked into the table, playing with the paper clips on the files in front of us, smiling sweetly. Good old Luc, I think, come on, let's get old grouch ready for Christmas. Who needs a meeting today of all days?! No one noticed the dragon slip under the large mahogany table, and the whole room seemed not to hear the rumble and notice movements by our feet. I am a bit disconcerted to have hot breath on my thigh as Lucy digs through the sweet jar she's been given, dropping jelly babies into an open mouth. Each one disappears with a satisfying smacking noise.

We are all having to justify our Christmas sales figures. My business results are poor. I know that, but we are a growth business, I try to argue. I am sweating, under attack. The CEO persists in his interrogation. Others in the team are slipping down in their seats, keeping out of the argument, one or two have tried to help me, but there is no stopping him. It was coming; of course, it was.

"I gave you a chance, gave you resources, listened to your proposals, accepted your part of the business might be different, but look at the results." He slaps the financial report on the table, and his face gets redder and redder as his anger rises. I knew it was coming. He hates this new business; it doesn't work how the rest of their business works. Now he's picking through some of my recent customer emails, which he normally ignores. He knows the company needs to change, but his shares are losing value, and we all know he wanted to cash out and retire this year.

> "No one noticed the dragon slip under the large mahogany table."

I need to fight back, but not with Lucy here, not today. She looks worried, peering up into my face and holding tightly to my little finger with her left hand. As she reaches into the sweet jar with her other hand, it tips. Before I can reach out, it starts to roll down the length of the table, coloured jelly babies tipping out – red, black, yellow, green. Everyone watches, transfixed, as it finally drops off the edge, just as the Finance Director makes a snatch at the disappearing jar. He leans over to pick up the container, then pulls back, fear on his face.

First, we see smoke, then the nose, then the teeth. The eyes appear, the flashing scales. The front feet haul up onto the Chippendale table, leaving deep scratches on the polished surface. His body, as he stretches, fills that end of the huge boardroom. His head crashes into the ornately plastered ceiling, and his tail knocks the coffee cups off the side cabinet. With a roar of anger, flames and smoke spurt from his nostrils. The heat scorches down the table, incinerating reports and notepads, wrecking laptops and phones. The flames destroy the smart, organised file in front of the CEO and then, with a flick, the last heat blackens his hair and softens his smart royal blue designer glasses, making them droop and distort his nose.

"The flames destroy the smart, organised file in front of the CEO."

No one moves. The CEO sits there stunned. The left lens on his glasses drops out into the ashes of his papers. Around the table, hands go to faces, and there are stifled giggles along with an "oh dear" and a "that was unfortunate." I don't wait. I push back my seat and, with Lucy trotting next to me and

Leadership Magic

the dragon behind, leave the smouldering room.

"Happy Christmas, everyone," I call over my shoulder. "Catch up on all this in the New Year. Or, in case I'm not here, enjoy all that new business coming soon from the actions in my area."

In the car park, I consider matters. "Hey, dragon, any chance of a lift home? I think maybe we'll leave the company car here."

The dragon bends his head to allow Lucy and me to slip onto his back. We lift off, waving to the warehouse staff as we glide into the cold clear blue sky.

Difference and Diversity – Building Something New

We all think we are open-minded, tolerant, and ahead of the curve on openness, equality and diversity. Yet many of us aren't. We prefer the status quo. We like our "garden," our way of doing things as it is. Even if sometimes, things aren't working well. There's a lot of safety and security in the known. Bringing something different is often welcomed at an intellectual level. Still, we can struggle to land emotionally when we have to change ourselves or our ways of working in an organisation.

It's a tough reflective journey to bring about change, particularly while keeping some things as they are. Many businesses must maintain results in a current market while developing customers in new areas. It can seem like a constant jarring as new ideas rub up against old established

Something's Moving in the Garden

ways of working. Often flashes of learning and insight come in painful moments when mistakes have been made, words spoken in a harmful way, or people are floundering about what is happening.

Are you trying to bring in something new somewhere? It should be easy, huh? You are often the "dragon in the garden" or the boardroom. The difference is welcomed until you "roar" – when you challenge the status quo – the "way we do things around here." Conflict can then come along pretty quickly. It usually isn't deliberate but may be inevitable. You must articulate your goals, be persistent and flexible, build alliances and constantly adapt your approaches. And if you are a leader, everyone will be watching how you deal with these situations and your ability to handle matters with equity and balance for all.

> "Often flashes of learning and insight come in painful moments when mistakes have been made, words spoken in a harmful way, or people are floundering."

Prompts and Actions

What happens when change arrives, which is different from the norm or from what was planned or expected for yourself or your business? Do you take a particular stance, attitude, or behaviour when someone is in your "vegetable patch"?

In the same way, what happens when you step on someone's "prized flowerbed"? Perhaps with a new idea, a better way of doing something?

If you are trying to develop a new idea, or make a change, what resources or support do you need to be successful, particularly if you are in a more traditional environment?

Where do you suspect you may have prejudice or bias? Where do these show themselves, and in what situations? Are they reflected across your broader organisation? What needs to happen now?

"All change, even very large and powerful change, begins when a few people start talking with one another about something they care about."

~ Margaret J. Wheatley, Author and Organisational Development Leader

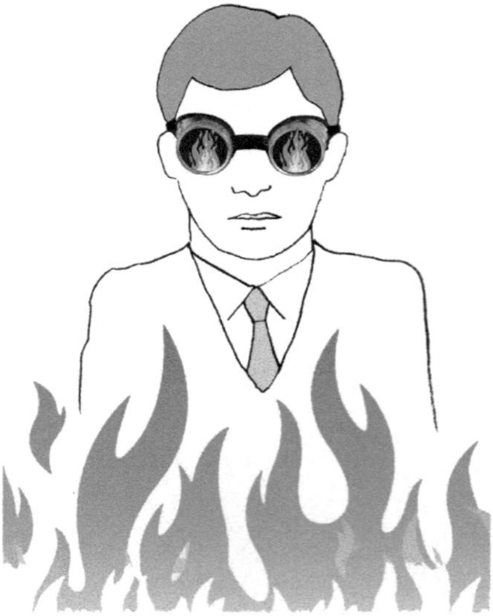

CHAPTER EIGHT
The Crucible

> Crucible conversations create a shift, a change to something better. We need to know our anchor points – why a discussion needs to happen, our approach and how we hold steady in the heat of this type of deeper dialogue.

"I should have done it a year ago. Why did I take so long?" It's a statement I have heard often, particularly from CEOs, about someone in a key executive position that's underperforming or behaving badly. Invariably when the situation is dealt with, it's in the best interests of everyone, but dealing with these issues isn't easy.

David, a senior leader, spent a long, frustrating time trying to resolve a situation with one of his top team – an executive who refused to change, who kept challenging the new strategy and not implementing team agreements. David spent endless time trying. Nothing changed until the CEO

Leadership Magic

had a more "real" conversation. A straight, honest appraisal of the situation.

The Crucible – Difficult Conversations

John adjusted his heat-reflective goggles, pulled on his steel-capped boots and slipped on his worn, blackened asbestos gloves. He smiled as he walked into the workshop, past the racks of new material, past the cooling stand, and on towards the roaring gas fire that reached up over six feet vertically. The noise boomed around the room. A huge crucible sat above the heat. As he climbed steps beside the flames, he looked over to the doorway. Coming reluctantly into the room were three people, walking awkwardly in their own heat suits. They, too, began ascending their own set of stairs on the other side of the crucible.

John took each step with energy and arrived under the metal edge. Putting one hand out, almost at a full arm's length, he curled his fingers around the lip. Remembering all his old rock-climbing skills, he swung his leg upwards in a wide arc, his foot hooked over the edge. With a graceful pull with his other hand, he flipped himself up and completely over and found himself in a wide circular dipping dish, almost the width of

> "Remembering all his old rock-climbing skills, he swung his leg upwards in a wide arc, his foot hooked over the edge."

The Crucible

a tennis court. At the centre, he could see the heat of the fire, fuelled by the huge Bunsen-style burner underneath, already turning the metal a blue-black colour as the crucible heated. Standing near the edge, his feet felt warm and cosy, although he knew that later they would be almost unbearably hot.

Across the dish, he saw the three visitors struggle over the edge themselves. They managed this by pushing, pulling and doing their best to help each other. One dropped a glove and watched it slide down the curve of the crucible and, arriving at the centre, begin to burn in the intense heat there. Trying not to look shocked, the man watched his glove shrivel, then pulled his face into a stoic, confident stare at John, who waved a hand in welcome and called across the space, "Hi there, welcome to the crucible. First time, hey?"

> "Stay near the outer edge until you can gauge the heat."

Three heads nod back, all with a similar smile. Unsure, yet seemingly confident and determined.

"Take care. Stay near the outer edge until you can gauge the heat. As you can see, the centre is very hot. Best avoided, but we may end up there. Let's see."

The man missing a glove took a step backwards and went to grip the edge of the crucible. He touched the metal with his bare hand and quickly pulled it away again. John carried on. "As I said, take care; this is a strange place for newcomers, but settle in, get a sense of how everything works, and you'll be fine."

Leadership Magic

With that, John sat down, using the lip of the dish as a handy seat. As he pulled his gauntlets further up his arms, he watched the three visitors slowly orientate themselves. They clearly found just standing difficult. Not due to the heat at this stage, but more the angle. Dipping both into the centre and off round the curve of the outside edge. This meant you had to bend one leg to remain upright. He watched as they practised the gangling walk. It reminded John again of his climbing trips, where the sheep neatly traversed the steep mountain slopes nimble and sure, with four legs seeming much easier than two.

> "We're here to talk about change. It's been slow or non-existent, which is why we ended up here. So, time for a different conversation."

"Okay, ready for a conversation," called John as he paced confidently towards the centre, where the red metal was glowing against the remaining black. "I'm John, You?"

"I'm Karl," said the one-glove man, turning slightly, "and this is Paul and Judy, who work for me." John raised his hand in welcome and pointed at his goggles. "Don't take them off. The heat dries out your eyes quickly and does terrible things to your eyelashes. I've seen some people lose them and even their eyebrows."

Paul, looking decidedly alarmed, nodded rapidly, his head bouncing up and down, which reflected the heat at the centre of the crucible in his glasses, creating an interesting rainbow effect. Judy just smiled and looked comfortable. She's been in

The Crucible

a crucible or two before, thought John. She'll handle this well.

"We're here to talk about change in your department. It's been slow or non-existent, which is why we ended up here. So, time for a different conversation."

"It's been fine as far as I'm concerned," retorted Karl, "Good enough or as good as the rest across the company. We're all just off-budget and have been for eighteen months now. If only the guys at head office would get their act together, we'd all be doing better." His face shaped into a smug "I've been here before" look. Paul opened his mouth to add something, got a glare and then a nudge in the ribs from Karl and bit his lip instead. Judy moved a few steps to the side as she watched John reach into his tunic pocket. In the flash of an eye, the hammer in his hand struck the crucible sending a ripple of vibration through the whole metal dish. Karl and Paul bounced forward, sliding a metre towards the centre. Judy, who intuitively was ready, stayed braced in the same position. John swung the hammer, ready to strike again.

"Woah man, woah," called Karl, looking distinctly worried. His right boot just touched the outer ring of the red circle of heat. The sweat dripped from his forehead and nose, landing with a hiss on the metal plate.

There were no more smiles from John. He had a determined look. They all watched as he spoke into a small radio clipped to his lapel. They noticed the roar of the heater beneath their feet rose to another level and watched as the metal went from red to white. John crossed his arms and looked at Karl, who was already back peddling up the slope.

Leadership Magic

"Sorry, Karl, but we need some change, fast change, and as Team Leader, it needs to come from you, not Paul or Judy. They follow your example." Karl looked at his boots gently smoking, the end of one lace already black and grizzled where it had made contact with the metal. Judy reached over to Paul and gently pulled him away up the slope, leaving John and Karl eyeing each other across the swirling heat.

"Okay, ready," said John softly and, leaning across the white heat, pulled Karl towards him. They met in the centre of the crucible, noses almost touching, an intense conversation taking place as the steam and smoke billowed around them, quickly enveloping them completely.

Judy and Paul, now back at the lip of the dish, looked down and just saw the two heads close together. Neither John nor Karl now had their goggles on. Both are intent on words being spoken, both ignoring the flames licking around them. Paul, now shaking and perspiring, gripped Judy's hand. She thought this very strange because mostly he either ignored her or made irritating stupid, or sarcastic comments. Judy took his hand off hers, rather like removing an unwelcome insect and placed it on the crucible lip. He fastened one, then two hands tightly onto the edge and sat down in an

The Crucible

ungainly heap, putting his face on top of his leather gloves. His body heaved and shook, and he seemed to diminish right before her. Judy realised just how pitiful he really was. His smart clothes, slick words, and strutting style gone. A part of him was unburnt but changing, something being left in the crucible too.

She patted him on the head, "Okay, boy, let's get down those stairs, get out of these stupid suits. Karl may need a stiff drink when he gets out of here. Or maybe a long cool glass of water when we see him next, assuming he does come back, of course." She smiled at this, then hopped over the crucible edge and disappeared down the stairs. She had stuff to get done back at the office and customers to call.

Difficult Conversations – Accepting the Temperature May Rise

This story comes out of several conversations at different times with leaders in a wide variety of organisations. After looking at the issue together, often about a key team member, we have prepared for a different type of discussion. A conversation where a significant shift is required from someone because there's an insurmountable block causing difficulty for everyone. Being willing to go into a crucible, a place of change, with another person seems to be at the centre of this resolution. There seems to be a need to go to a new place of emotional heat and intense conversation,

Leadership Magic

where things can melt and reform. A shift, when things which perhaps didn't seem possible before can happen. A moment of truth and sometimes brutal honesty.

A crucible, though, isn't always an easy place to be, as, of course, the analogy is all about different, direct dialogue. Sometimes just awkward and tricky, words not spoken before. Sometimes, almost unbearable, particularly in the face of the other person's strong emotions, or indeed our own. Facing key issues and questions requires strong personal leadership and sure anchor points within us – why we are doing this, what is the issue, how this needs to change – to ensure we can take ourselves and others through this heat of change.

> "Being willing to go into a crucible, a place of change, with another person seems to be at the centre of this resolution."

I have witnessed many leaders vacillate around difficult discussions. Then finally, when they have taken the plunge, the result afterwards has an upsurge in energy and direction and accelerated change. "I should have done this months or years ago," they say. Maybe they should have, but I am very respectful of the time and strength this takes. These are not easy conversations. They significantly impact individuals and the organisation, but they are at the core of good leadership.

The Crucible

Prompts and Actions

Do you have a situation that requires a "crucible" type of conversation? How can you approach this knowing there will be history, emotion, probably bias on both sides and very strong opinions?

What does this conversation require of you? What anchor points do you have – what information and examples do you have that take the discussion away from opinion and personality toward fact?

As you enter a crucible, what is the best result for you and the other person?

How do you ensure the conversation is held with dignity and integrity for each party involved?

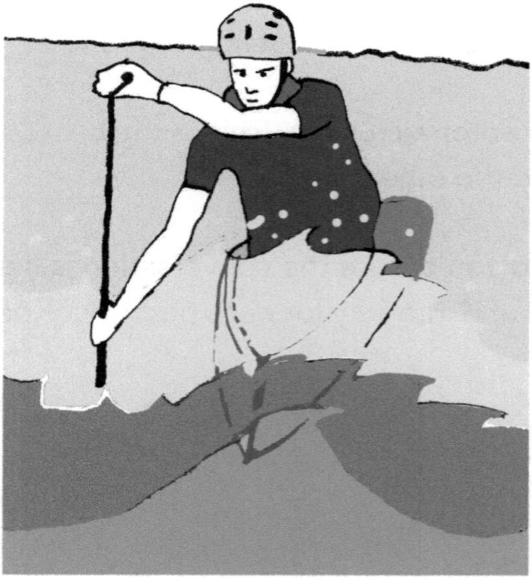

CHAPTER NINE

Canoe Trip

> Make plans and get experts to help. Then when you are underway, work with what is actually happening. Know when to push through and keep going and when to back off and refocus.

This story started me writing about situations and finding the impact of reflection through storytelling. It allowed me to look at a situation I'd experienced and reshape some of my fear and concern in a new way. It gave me the space to look at the change in a different way. And, sometimes, as in this story, we find ourselves in change and just have to go through it, even if it is tough and scary. I still don't find change that easy even after all these years, but my experience tells me – you can get through it!

Canoe Trip: Expecting Change

The warm evening air cooled as it met the surface of the river, the rings made by the fish barely disturbing the water as the sun started to slip beneath the horizon. The three young men stood on the bank, watching the current flowing. Two looked slightly bored, one happy.

"No problem here," said Clive. "Straight forward until you get to that point down there."

"Where?" I asked, already feeling the fear begin to well up inside me.

"Just a dink left then right. Keep your canoe steady, and you're through," said Chris leaning back on the tree, his usual relaxed, eloquent and clear self.

Here we were with a free day, no work at the outdoor pursuit centre, so the three of us were off canoeing together. Clive, Chief Instructor, is strong, muscular and losing hair on top already. A diamond-shaped body, all shoulders, broad chest which slips away in the bottom half. Just as well, or he wouldn't fit into that sleek canoe of his.

Chris, Assistant Chief Instructor, large afro hair spilling over his shoulders, strong London accent, down-to-earth, very capable. And, of course, me. How did I end up teaching outdoor pursuits? Who knows. I loved climbing and caving but felt ambivalent about canoeing – well, probably to water in general. I'm not much of a swimmer.

We climb back into the rusty van. I think I can handle this. Only one tricky bit on the route we've chosen, and I'm guessing they're thinking: "Not much excitement here,

Canoe Trip

routine practice drill." Oh well. I settle back on the grubby plastic seat. Chris drives us to the pub as the rain begins to spatter on the windscreen.

The driving rain wakes me up. It's already seeping through the rotten window, pooling on the shelf. I move my three books to a safer spot and look out. Yesterday's beautiful day is a memory, as the rain shoots up the valley and batters into the bunkhouse. Huge puddles have already formed in the field, and two vehicles in the car park have a running stream flowing between them. I relax, breathe, sigh deeply and pull the bedclothes over my head. I know it's off – too much rain.

As I relax, just thinking about the next chapter of the new novel I bought in Swansea last week, they both bang on the door together. A triumphant wallop rattles the already loose door.

"Come on, let's go. It's looking great out there." The pleasure in their voices boomed into the bedroom. Can't I just duck out, I think. Let them have their moment? But it doesn't work like that here. We test ourselves and train together even on days off. So, an hour later, we're loading canoes up onto the roof of the minibus, the rain sliding down my forearms and running right down to my shoulders before soaking into my shirt.

Brian's here now. Our chef and sort of centre organiser. He's a good cook but also has "cook mood swings." Last week he spent the last of the budget on new plants for the centre. For twenty-four hours, we admired our new greenery, then someone left the door open and in came the two goats. They

Leadership Magic

ate each plant down to a stalk, then made their way into the office and ate all the papers on the notice board, leaving a tideline of ragged paper where they could just reach. Brian hit a rage, at the goats, at us for someone leaving the door open and went on the booze for twenty-four hours. We're just about family, so it's fine, and there's no in-group. So, we cobble meals together for a day or so.

Brian's our driver for the day. He's on a high, big smile, humming a tune from the radio. Well, he would be – all he's doing is driving. He's in the van now while we struggle tying knots in the rain. We climb aboard, and the rain thunders on the roof. There's one singing chef, two smiling senior instructors – rubbing at windows and pointing out changes the rain is making to the landscape – and me, crumbled down in the plastic seat, feeling sorry for myself.

> "What's different is the river. It's gone from a clear, slow-moving, gentle gliding pool to a raging, brown, frothy, rushing maelstrom."

It's no better after half an hour when we arrive at the drop-off point. The rain continues to fall. What's different is the river. It's gone from a clear, slow-moving, gentle gliding pool to a raging, brown, frothy, rushing maelstrom. The chef looks frightened. I *am* frightened. Clive and Chris's eyes light up.

"Let's go," they shout and almost fall off the bus in their hurry to be on the water. My heart is beating. Breathe, I say to myself. It's only water. You're with the two best canoeists, you know. It'll be fine. I push myself off my safe plastic seat

Canoe Trip

and squeeze Brian's shoulder, he gives me the thumbs up, and I'm out in the rain.

On the river we go, the three canoes pulled by the current. It's moving fast. We know the drill, though, and Clive's shouting through the rain. "Usual stuff. Follow me. Chris, bring up the rear."

We are swept along the river, touching paddles to maintain direction. I wonder how long it will take to get to the estuary at this speed. We're only doing two miles, though, so it'll be a quick trip at this rate. I see Brian speeding along the road, glimpses of the van occasionally flashing through the trees. He's getting ahead to the pull-out point. I'm okay. I might even be enjoying myself as I listen to the rhythmic slap of the paddles on the water. I watch the occasional log outpace us, and I wave to a morose, wet heron perched on a stump.

We sweep around the corner heading to the only difficult bit. Where is it? I see only waves, big waves. The dink right, dink left have disappeared; there is no dink at all. I hear Clive mutter ahead of me, then turn his head and shout, "Paddle, paddle, paddle like fuck."

I do. We all do. The blades drive into the river. We're pacing through the water now with no way back. Already the waves are building. "Bang!" as the boats rise on the up. "Bang!" on the waves as we crash on the downside. My arms are aching already. I glance to my left. Chris is hit by a rogue wave, and he's over. "Roll, Chris, roll!" Can he do it in this water? He's a master at it usually.

I look ahead. "Where's Clive?" He's over too. I see his canoe

Leadership Magic

upside down, the end of his blade swishing out of the water as he fights to get upright.

"Fuck, Fuck, paddle, paddle, fuck, fuck, paddle, paddle," I shout as I hit the now-defunct double dink. Up the wave. There's no top. It must be ten feet tall. Down the other side. "Paddle, paddle, fuck fuck." The nose of the canoe dives into the water. My shoulders heave, the muscles screaming as I haul forward through the next wave. Water is everywhere. I can't see. It's brown, tasting of soil. It's in my mouth, pouring over me. The paddle stops working; there's no air to lift in. I try anyway. Then I'm out, still swirling my paddle like crazy, still shouting my mantra, "Paddle, paddle, fuck, fuck."

> "The nose of the canoe dives into the water. My shoulders heave, the muscles screaming as I haul forward through the next wave. Water is everywhere. I can't see."

I hear the cheering before I see him. Brian is up on the swing bridge ahead, right in the middle. Leaning over, whooping, "That a boy, yeah man, whoo, whoo, whoo." I want to raise my hand, do a clenched fist or something, but my hands are clamped to the hand grips on the paddle. My knuckles are white, locked in place. I sweep down towards him. He's hopping on one foot, doing a jig, still whooping and clapping. And then I'm under the bridge and gone. "Cool!" he shouts, "Cool!"

Clive found me a few minutes later. My arms wrapped around a tree at the side of the river. He was white. I was white. I was shaking, my whole body shaking, wanting to be sick,

Canoe Trip

wanting out of the boat. "I thought you'd drowned," he said quietly as Chris swept in behind him, doing a smart stop at the riverbank. I shook my head. Hugged my tree and smiled. We all smiled.

Managing Change and Persisting

Change isn't easy. Well, for some, yes. For others like me, it is a tricky customer. Things shift, the thought-through plan goes out of the window as the action starts, and sometimes it isn't possible to stop; you just have to keep going. There may be support around you; there may not. You may not even know you are doing the right thing in the right way but stepping one foot in front of another (or one paddle blade) and persisting takes you somewhere.

The most successful leaders I know keep going; they persist and demand that others persist, even when conditions are against them, or people cannot see or even sense the finishing line. This means trusting yourself, relying on your own judgement and managing yourself. Situations do change, rivers do flood, and yes, sometimes we need to get off the water and regroup. Other times we just have to keep going. Even when the experts are absent, leaving you without a guide, you can get there.

"Situations do change, rivers do flood, and yes, sometimes, we need to get off the water and regroup. Other times we just have to keep going."

Prompts and Actions

How are you with change, particularly when you are not fully in control of that change? How do you react? How do you manage? What is your inner and outer reaction?

When circumstances shift, how flexible are you? Do you need to "bash" your way through sometimes? What is your level of commitment and willingness to battle through?

Who is there to encourage you? Who is your most enthusiastic supporter? Who will also challenge you and give you straight feedback to get you back on track?

In the same way, how can you encourage others through change?

> "No one knows for sure what is out there. That's why we keep looking. Keep your faith, travel hopefully. The universe will surprise you constantly."
>
> ~ Jodie Whittaker, Doctor Who, BBC

FINAL THOUGHTS

A Day at the Office

I sit looking at the blank screen, shifting uncomfortably in my chair. Buddy, the cocker spaniel, is curled up on his bed under the desk snoring gently, occasionally shaking and making squeaking noises as he chases rabbits in his dreams. It's another day in the home office for him. I touch the keyboard, pull my hands away, look around, think about a second coffee and wonder about checking my mail. Then a moment of inspiration and clarity arrives. I can see a starting point. I feel a smile on my face. Fingers begin tapping. An opening sentence of the final part of this story begins to appear . . .

Enjoy Your Journey – Create the Story You Want

Time is short. Days can whiz past and seem to speed up as you get older; I can testify to that. So, enjoy your own evolving journey and seize as many moments as you can. Take the opportunities, then store those events in your memory bank for sustenance later. Sometimes you may have to work at this and remember to seize those moments – to take action, to move, to push a bit, to go the extra mile to shape your story a little. Or perhaps it's the opposite – maybe some days you just need to sit in the sun, relax, or spend time with people you love and care about. I have a powerful memory from a time in my twenties of just that, and it is my criteria for happiness even now.

Importantly though, create your own story. The one you want. In fact, use storytelling to guide and help you. Stop occasionally and just write . . . even if you think you can't. Things honestly do clarify when you write your thoughts down on paper or on a screen. And if "just write" is difficult, try the fable-style route like me. Our imagination wants to help. "Once upon a time" works for a very good reason, as mythical or imaginary characters can often open the space in front of us, the path forward – they love an adventure!

> Create your own story. The one you want.

The slightly off-the-wall stories I shared in this book got me into writing and held me there. Despite thoughts of "I can't write, and my English is terrible" (I still have shocking spelling), my interest in the subject and the journey happening inside the narrative made me persist. Even when I could hear those internal doubts banging a drum loudly inside me, telling me to stop. So, ask those demons to hold off, just start, and then persevere. Something new will begin to appear as you write, or speak out, that opening sentence.

A Day at the Office

It works; it really does. And doing this might just give you a new perspective on a key question or an issue you are facing. That's happened so often to me, I find it exciting as it appears each time. Creating a story will take you forwards – honestly, it will. So go on, let your imagination help you, write that first sentence – then push on and find the hero or heroine in your story and all those other wonderful details – Who are the villains? Who solves the problem? What sets you up for success? Where is the treasure hidden? and much more.

Enjoy yourself, and you might just end up with a powerful story which could tilt your world a little differently and show you new and interesting ways forward.

My very best wishes
Grahame

ACKNOWLEDGEMENTS

To Barbara for her support and encouragement to write – check out her creative writing workshops on www.freefall.com

To my family, Sue, Joe, Rebecca and Jack for their wonderful support throughout.

To John Cormode, Les Wicks, Jo Howard, Bob Gorzynski, Graham Prentice and Cindy Rampersaud for reading the stories and drafts, making suggestions, nudging, challenging, encouraging and keeping me at it.

To Marcus Bolt for the illustrations, Sandy Draper for editing, Jim Baker for proofreading and Cath Murray for the layout and overall design.

To all my clients and friends across the years, who have provided me with such rich material to write about.

You are all true stars, everyone of you . . . thank you.

ABOUT THE AUTHOR

I am a coach and facilitator working with all sorts of organisations, large and small. Some are well known, like Google, Tetra Pak, PricewaterhouseCoopers, Costa Coffee, Beko, and Pearson, through to medium size businesses and small entrepreneurial start-ups and charities.

My work is always in partnership with the senior executive. Together we build the change they are looking for in themselves or their organisation. I have a creative background and a different psychology from many of the people I work with. This difference often creates something new and interesting as we work together.

In my downtime, I write (phew, you got this far, thank you!), work in wood (my original training was in furniture design), play tennis, sing in a community choir, play the sax and guitar (poorly) and walk our cocker spaniel. I'm married (God bless Sue as I struggled to bring this book to life), have three grown children who have flown the nest, and now I am old enough to even be a grandparent.